REFUGEE HERITAGE

Refugee Heritage
Published by Refugee Radio
Registered charity: 1133554
www.refugeeradio.org.uk

This edition 2023
Copyright © Refugee Radio 2022
First printed October 2022

ISBN-13: 978-0-9929374-4-7

Refugee Heritage:
An Oral History of Asylum

Stephen Silverwood

Refugee Radio is a charity supporting people who have been forced to flee their homes because of war and persecution. In addition to our radio programme, we also run different projects in the community such as our weekly mental-health support group and our specialist casework advice project.

www.refugeeradio.org.uk

Conversation Over Borders is a Community Interest Company (CIC). We are a team hundreds strong of volunteers and learners, Coordinators and Content Creators, Teaching Consultants and Wellbeing Officers, headed up by our Board of Advisors and Directors. We connect asylum seekers & refugees with volunteer tutors for free one-on-one online English conversation classes.

www.conversationoverborders.org

Acknowledgements

This book is based on oral-history interviews with refugees and asylum seekers living in Brighton and beyond. Most of the interviews were conducted as part of the Refugee Heritage project, which was a joint initiative between Refugee Radio and Conversation Over Borders. The project was made possible by the generosity of the Heritage Lottery Fund and by the invaluable support of our volunteers who helped to conduct the interviews and to produce the accompanying documentary:

Alex Evangelou
Alex Hyne
Anna Scott
Daisy Wingate-Saul
Farah Mohebati
Henry Tydeman
Jasmine Cousins
Maria Wardale
Ottilie Carter
Rami Mansour
Rhiannon Amery
Rungroj Park Rojanachotikul
Sarah Warbrick

Proofreading and editorial assistance by Anna Scott and Colette Batten-Turner. Photos by Daisy Wingate-Saul. Accompanying documentary film produced by Colette Batten-Turner. The interviews were transcribed and edited into this book with notes by Stephen Silverwood.

Also by Refugee Radio Books:

Castaway Heritage (2019)

Takeaway Heritage (2016)

Refugee Radio Times (2014)

Note on the text

Some of the material in this book covers topics such as war, torture and sexual violence, which may be disturbing. We believe that it is important to share people's life stories and oral histories exactly as they have been presented to us and have not removed any of this content.

All of the quotes are based on verbatim transcripts from oral-history life-story interviews and have not been overly edited into standard English. We have adopted this approach in order to preserve the sound of each speaker's individual voice as faithfully as possible. We all use grammar differently when we are speaking, as opposed to when we are writing, and people who have different first languages will construct English in different ways. We felt that strictly correcting everyone's syntax would just airbrush out all of these interesting differences and would not stay true to the people speaking.

Full versions of these and other interviews can be streamed or downloaded at the Refugee Radio website, where you can also view the accompanying documentary film: www.refugeeradio.org.uk

Contents

Part One: Country of Origin

Part Two: Living in Limbo

Part Three: Life in the UK

Respondent	Country of Origin
Ali	Egypt
Aston	Central Africa
August	Uganda
Daryan	Middle East
Edgar	Central Africa
Gabriel	Central Africa
Haddy	West Africa
Idris	Kenya
Jay	Cameroon
John	Cameroon
June	North Africa
Kajoli	Bangladesh
Mima	Burma
Mo	Syria
Mostafa	North Africa
Oba	West Africa
Patience	Cameroon
Paul	East Africa
Reyhan	East Turkistan (China)
Rose	Southern Africa
Saleh	Middle East
Samson	Southern Africa
Yasmin	Iran
Yezda	Kurdistan (Syria)
Yusef	Eritrea
Zula	Eritrea

Names have been changed to anonymise the respondents and protect their identities. We have indicated the general region instead of the country of origin for each speaker, unless they have specified it in their text, in order to give some indication of where they are from without compromising their anonymity.

Part One: Country of Origin

"If you just speak with me one word, you will hear a million words back."
Saleh.

Country of Origin- Notes

Why start with "Country of Origin"? Because the story always does.

The phrase itself comes from the 1951 Geneva Convention: a refugee is someone who is "unable or unwilling to return to their country of origin owing to a well-founded fear of being persecuted for reasons of race, religion, nationality, membership of a particular social group, or political opinion."

This book is divided into three parts according to the structure of the asylum journey: we travel with our respondents from their early lives in their home countries, through their problems with the authorities, their flight to the UK, the long process of claiming asylum and the quest for refugee status.

But everything begins back home. Even when someone has progressed through every stage of the asylum journey, it is all within the context of the motherland and what that means to each individual. Our respondent, Yusef, tells us later in this book that, for him, it is not so much about becoming British as it is resisting the process of unbecoming Eritrean. To understand the life of a refugee, we must first understand their life before that label was put upon them.

"Where are you from?" is a question that is very familiar to our clients at the Refugee Radio charity. It is a question that will be familiar to any person of colour in the UK, often followed up with, "No, but where are you really from?" if the first answer fails to satisfy. The writer, Afua Hirsch, describes what they call The Question as, "The most persistent reminder of that sense of not belonging." Vanessa Hua writes that the people who ask her The Question are, "Pleased to confirm their suspicion that my family isn't from here, that [my family] are perpetual foreigners." The journalist, Rakshitha Arni Ravishankar, asserts that the intention behind The Question is critical: "Why am I even asking this question? What do I hope to gain from this specific question, as opposed to, say, asking someone about their favourite holiday destination or music band?"

In her memoir (Bossypants, 2011) the actress Tina Fey writes about the scar on her chin. She recounts that she was playing outside her house one day when a random stranger slashed her across the face with a knife. She was five years old. There was no reason behind the attack and they never caught the man. Fey writes that she has always been able to tell a lot about people by whether they ask her about her scar, and in particular how quickly they ask her about her scar. If it comes up naturally somehow, she might share the story, but, she writes: "There's another sort of person who thinks it makes them seem brave or sensitive or wonderfully direct to ask me about it right away […] My whole life, people who ask about my scar within one week of knowing me have invariably turned out to be egomaniacs of average intelligence or less."

The intention behind The Question is generally revealed in the follow-up question. We had a client who was being deported to South Africa, and when I visited her in the removal centre she said that strangers would often ask her where she was from, but when she told them they would either just shrug and walk away, or reply, "Oh, Africa! Like in the Lion King?"

For many questioners, the intention behind The Question is simply to resolve a mental discomfort about not being able to easily categorise you. As soon as you are neatly filed away in the right box, they can go back to forgetting you exist.

When you apply for asylum, you have to go to the Home Office and plead your case with the UK Border Agency (UKBA) at an Asylum Intake Unit by explaining why it is not safe for you to go back home. In order to determine whether your story is accurate, the UKBA maintains a Country of Origin Information Service that produces reports on what they call the main asylum-producing countries. The only problem is that the reports themselves are not always accurate and the Home Office decision-makers use the information very selectively, often twisting it to their needs or in some cases simply just making it up (as detailed in the report of the Independent Chief Inspector of the UKBA in 2011). Reports by other agencies such as the UNHCR, Human Rights Watch, and even the CIA, are much more reliable. The Home Office does not want to know.

Many asylum cases are rejected before they have started, simply because the applicant had the wrong country of origin in the first place. In 1995, then-Home Secretary, Michael 'Something of the Night' Howard, published the first list of countries that you could not claim asylum from: India, Pakistan, Ghana, Bulgaria, Cyprus, Poland and Romania. Opponents accused him of playing the race card. Howard went and named it the White List.

In 2003, then-Home Secretary, David 'Nanny's Visa' Blunkett, added more: Albania, Jamaica, Macedonia, Moldova and Serbia/Montenegro. By the time of writing, even more orders were in force in relation to: Bolivia, Brazil, Ecuador, South Africa, Kosovo, Mongolia, Bosnia-Herzegovina, Mauritius, Peru, South Korea, Ghana, Nigeria, Gambia, Kenya, Liberia, Malawi, Mali and Sierra Leone. Bangladesh, Jamaica and Ukraine are also still technically on the list. There are widely-reported human rights issues in many of these countries, especially around the treatment of ethnic minorities and people who are LGBTQ. There are well-documented uses of torture, extrajudicial killings and the suppression of the press. The Home Office does not want to know. It is quite ready to remove people back to countries where known persecution exists.

The Question, then, can be a matter of life or death.

So let's have a look at the most common countries of origin for asylum applications to the UK over the last thirty years:

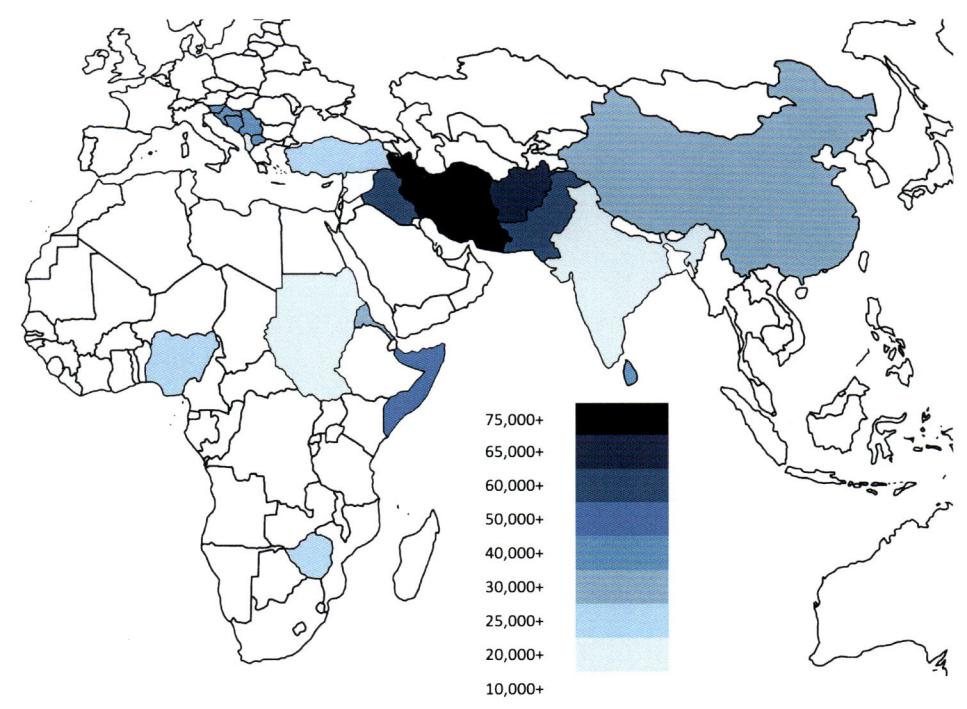

75,000+

65,000+

60,000+

50,000+

40,000+

30,000+

25,000+

20,000+

10,000+

Country of origin for asylum applications in the UK 1992-2022

Country of Origin	Applications for asylum in the UK 1992–2022
Iran	76,113
Afghanistan	67,664
Pakistan	62,462
Iraq	60,410
Somalia	59,106
Sri Lanka	47,742
FRY	42,190
Eritrea	35,726
China	32,946
Zimbabwe	28,271
Turkey	27,118
Nigeria	26,660
India	25,486
Albania	25,243
Sudan	20,554
Syria	14,773
Bangladesh	2,532

(Figures from our analysis of Home Office asylum and resettlement datasheets from Quarter 1, 1999 up to Quarter 2, 2022).

Many of these are countries that have been blighted by war and other armed conflicts: Afghanistan, Iraq, Somalia, Sri Lanka, Sudan, Syria etc.

Others are characterised by their poor human rights records, such as China and Iran.

According to the 2022 Human Rights Watch country report, Iran is one of the world's leading implementers of the death penalty, executing hundreds of people every year; Iranian security forces have responded to recent protests with excessive force, including murdering women for breaking hijab rules; Iranian authorities restrict freedom of the press and freedom of expression; Iran harasses and detains human rights lawyers and other defenders; the Iranian courts rely on confessions obtained under torture as evidence; the law discriminates against Baha'is and other religious minorities and denies freedom of worship; the law also discriminates against women in a range of matters, and this year another woman was sentenced to death by stoning for an allegation of adultery.

The UK is the largest recipient of Iranian asylum claims in Europe- there were more than 10,446 new applications in the UK last year as opposed to Germany (2,693) and Canada (1,396), the next biggest asylum destinations. Most of the people crossing the English Channel in small boats recently have been Iraqis and Iranians. The reasons why Iranians would want to come to the UK specifically are varied, but historically the trend began with Iranians fleeing the Islamic revolution after the fall of the Shah in the 1970s. Migratory flows tend to follow routes established over time, as those who have gone ahead send back positive messages. Statistically, Iranian asylum claims are also more likely to be successful in the UK than in Germany or France.

However, this obscures other parts of the picture such as the number of Iranian refugees living in Turkey (official figures vary between 40,000-126,000). Only a small percentage of these people have formally claimed asylum there, and this may be due to the danger of living openly in such close proximity to Tehran. In recent years, operatives of the Islamic Republic have taken action against Iranian refugees in Turkey- including people being beaten and shot. In some cases people have been kidnapped off the streets of Turkey and taken back to Iran to be jailed by the secret police.

It is worth noting that the number of Iranians in the UK is only a fraction of the total emigration from Iran. According to the 2021 Census, there are 37,000 Iranian nationals resident in the UK, while the ONS estimates the total Iranian-born population to be 70,000. This is less than 2% of the 4,000,000 Iranians living in exile worldwide (Ministry of Foreign Affairs of Iran 2021 statistics).

It is also worth noting that the number of Iranians in the UK is only a fraction of immigration to the UK as a whole: they make up less than 1% of the total number of people living in the UK who were born abroad (House of Commons Library 2022 migration statistics).

The global picture for countries of origin is quite different to that of UK refugees:

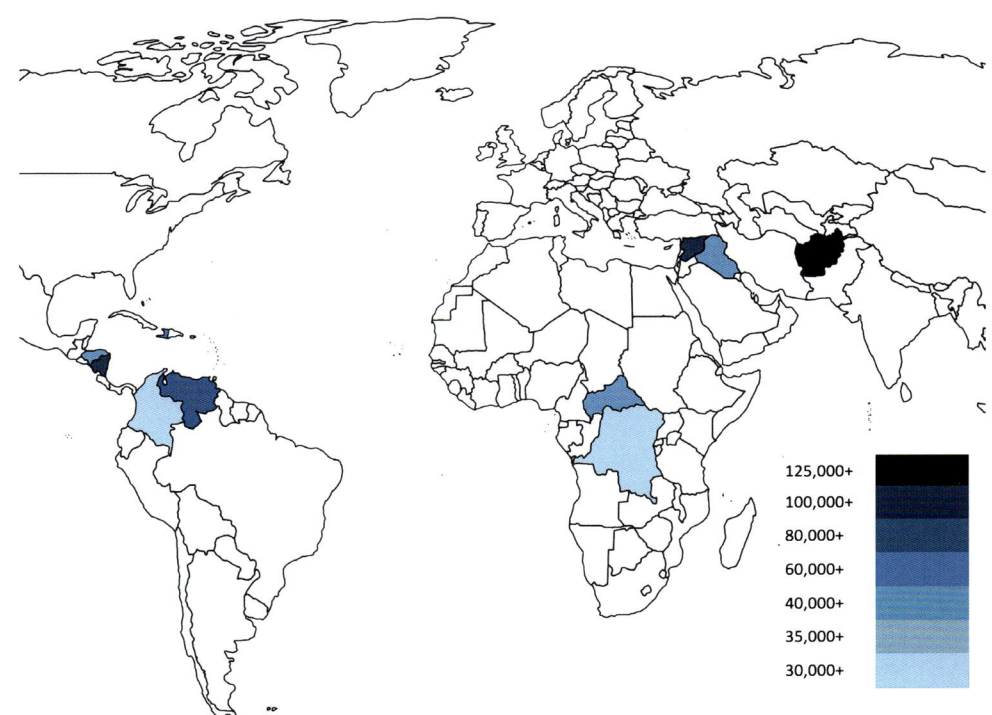

Country of origin for asylum applications worldwide UK 2021

Country of Origin	Applications for asylum worldwide in 2021
Afghanistan	125,483
Syria	109,790
Nicaragua	108,475
Venezuela	87,977
Haiti	64,640
Central African Republic	47,782
Honduras	47,248
Iraq	37,667
DRC	33,015
Colombia	31,281

(Worldata 2021).

Afghanistan, Syria and Iraq are still present in the global rankings, but many of the others from the UK list have fallen off in favour of countries from South and Central America.

Pakistan, which is the third most common country of origin for asylum applicants in the UK, does not even feature in the global rankings at all.

The most common destination last year for people from Pakistan was Italy, which had a 92% rejection rate, and Greece, where the rate was over 95%.

85% of asylum claims from Pakistan are refused in the UK (Home Office statistics 2017), mostly on the basis that there is supposedly a functioning criminal justice system in the country of origin. And yet the Home Office's own policy guidance on Pakistan states that the police there are the most corrupt institution in the country, and refers to arbitrary arrest and detention, torture, broken courts and extrajudicial killings as commonplace. The Home Office recognises that members of the minority Ahmadi religious community face restrictive legislation, persecution and a lack of state protection, but when Ahmadi people seek asylum, the Home Office often claims that they are just pretending to be Ahmadi. The same is true for Christian converts and people who have been persecuted for their sexuality. And then, even if the Home Office does believe them, it will refuse the claim anyway because "internal relocation may be both relevant and reasonable" i.e. it thinks that you should just move to another place within the country and everything will be fine. Which, of course, is not how countries generally work.

The vast majority of refugees displaced abroad are living in a neighbouring country to their homeland, often in camps around the border. According to the UNHRC, the figure is at least 72%. This includes groups like the 800,000 Rohingya living in shanty camps in Bangladesh and the 175,000 Saharawis ousted by Morocco into the Saharan desert. Around a quarter of the world's refugees live in camps- more than 6,500,000 people in total. Most of these people will not go through a formal asylum process under the Geneva convention, but let's take a look at the most common destinations for those countries where people do formally apply:

Destination	Applications for asylum 2021
Germany	148,159
Mexico	131,194
United States	117,490
Costa Rica	108,712
France	89,354
Spain	65,301
United Kingdom	56,367
Italy	53,055
DRC	45,866
Uganda	41,801

(Worlddata 2021).

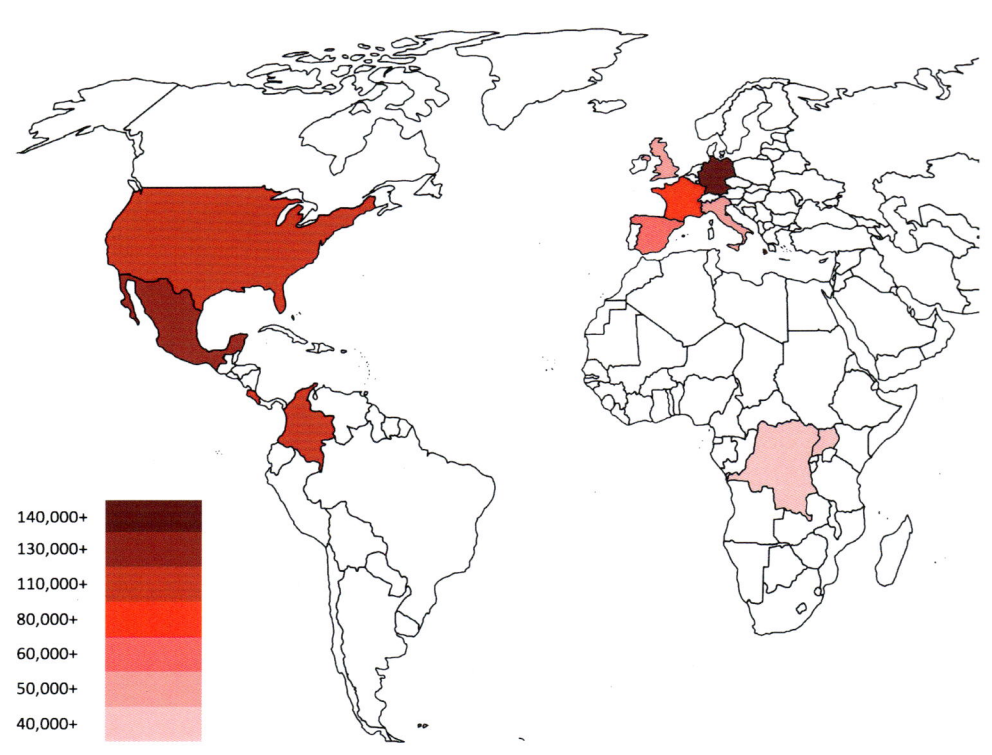

140,000+	
130,000+	
110,000+	
80,000+	
60,000+	
50,000+	
40,000+	

Most common destinations for formal asylum applications 2021

The numbers for the top three countries for formal asylum applications (see above) are dwarfed by the total number of refugees in the major hosting countries (see to the right), many of whom have been there for years without status:

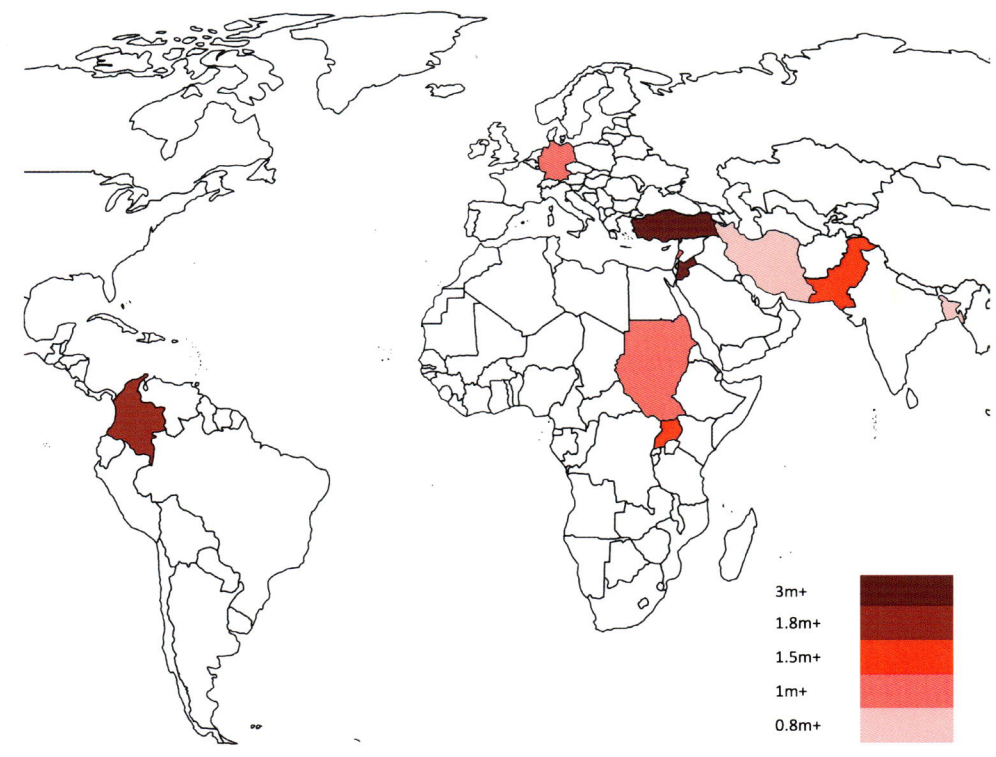

Number of refugees in the major hosting countries 2021

Major hosting countries	Number of refugees hosted
Turkey	3.8m
Jordan	3.02m
Colombia	1.8m
Uganda	1.5m
Pakistan	1.5m
Lebanon	1.33m
Germany	1.3m
Sudan	1.06m
Bangladesh	0.88m
Iran	0.8m

(Source: UNHRC statistics 2021)

These figures do not yet include data on Russia's invasion of Ukraine in 2022, which resulted in an exodus of 4.8m international refugees and a further 7.1m internally displaced people.

Turkey and Pakistan are both oddities in that they feature in the list of major hosting countries for refugees and also in the list of most common countries of origin for UK asylum applications. In the case of Pakistan, these are overwhelmingly Afghan refugees, while for Turkey they are mostly refugees from Syria, both of which also feature in the UK list.

The Democratic Republic of Congo (DRC) features in the list of top asylum-producing countries as well as the list of top destinations for formal asylum claims (where it appears besides Uganda). The situation is complex, with 5.5m people internally displaced within the DRC alongside 500,000 refugees from neighbouring Burundi, South Sudan and the Central African Republic. There are a number of armed conflicts in the DRC, including the genocidal persecution of the Banyamulenge in the Kivu region.

In summary then, it is crucial for us to begin our story in the country of origin. We must locate each voice in the context of home in order to understand the patterns of international movement and the meaning behind individual journeys.

The narrative begins with the microcosm of childhood and the early years.

Early years

I started seeing injustices when I was a young boy.

My papa died when I was twelve. My dad was an academic and we had everything that we needed when I was growing up. But when my dad died, we took a nosedive to poverty. And of course, growing up was not fun. And that is when I started seeing injustices because we lost everything that my dad had. Then it was just us and our mum.

So I started asking myself, alright- my dad had this car, where did it go? My dad had this house, where did it go? And then my mum had difficulty explaining certain things to us. And that is when I started asking: how is this possible that these things can be happening? So I started fighting for injustice from that young age.

It is said that I became a rebel when I was around twelve years old.

Idris (Kenya)

As a child, I just wanted to enjoy my childhood life with my brothers and sister and friends. I didn't want to know what was going on with my people until I saw a dead body, when me and my brothers and sister we were playing by a river bank. The dead body was so badly decomposed and smells so bad. So we were just so terrified to see the dead body. And we ran back home and we asked our Father to go down to the river and see that body; and my father removed that body. But we were just still terrified and asked my father: why this dead body was here at our playground by the riverbank?

My father said there was a village upstream, and the Burmese army often came to the village. They grabbed villagers, farmers, and they forced them to work for them as a slave. These villagers, they were forced to carry heavy loads and military supplies for the troops, and the soldiers didn't give them proper rest and food and water. And when they couldn't work any longer, they were tortured and beaten into death, and their bodies were thrown in the river.

We were so scared. We couldn't go back to that playing ground for a long time.

Mima (Burma)

When I born my mum didn't find me a birth certificate. She told me, "You born when the British people leave my country and come back to the UK." I was born around that time, when we got our independence.

At that time I got one man, he was an old man. Asked that man the date and that man said to me, it's on the twenty fourth of May. He give me that date. That's why I used that date for my date of birth. But I don't know exactly the date. I don't know. My life is that.

Haddy (West Africa)

My mum is one of the strongest persons I know, and very hardworking. She had eight children in rural Africa. She brought us all up and she took us all to school, even when people were saying, "No, no, no, no, no, you can take these boys. But the girls? Leave it all alone!"

But she said, "No, no, no, no. Even if the girls are going to get married, I am taking them to school so that when they get married, they are going to be own persons, not their husbands persons. They are going to be independent individuals. So that's why I'm doing this."

And it's taught me a lot. It's taught me a lot: her reasoning and the way she saw things.

Idris

When I was young I would see somebody's family, people who live with their mum and their dad, but I didn't see my mum. I stayed with my aunties, and they make me do the whole job in the house. My hands they always dry because of the work I had to do. It's corns everywhere because I went through that.

So that time I didn't see my mum. I lived with my aunties and they used me. If anybody has a job in their homes, they don't use *their* children, they asked *me* to do that. Because my mum is not there.

I don't remember my age or anything, because when you have a lot of pains from when you're young till you get older, that trauma is in your head. Before you have your rape. Because no one looked after me, that's why my cousin raped me.

Haddy

My dream was in my childhood that my life would be in America, because I have been bullied all my life's childhood. I was not good-looking. All these making me... I was only six years old. I saw a dream my life will be in America: free moving, I can quit job, I don't have any problem. But it is every woman has a dream, has a fairy tale! They wants to become a Europe or western country because women can move freely, and in Bangladesh is no way.

Everything is controlled in our patriarchy power, so women can be how beautiful, how talented, it doesn't matter to them. If you are over-talented then no one can marry you! Something like all these, we just watching, but still you didn't realise women life can be that hard.

When I was that situation, it's same what am I divorce, marriage, live, divorce, what happened to me, it same happened with my mum, it same happened with my sister, so the same happened with my family. It's all women, and we are quite big family, and most are women and all have same story. And I was seeing all this and there is no boys, and just I knew I had to leave the place.

When I decided I would like to come here to the UK, this is not easy. Everyone can't come UK or America or Canada or any other country. It's not easy. You have to be very wealthy. But I came here I don't have a wealthy family. My father used to be a rich man, but when I born my father became a poor.

Still, we grew up very culturally, education, manner.

My mum is very feminist. My father is very like patriarchy power- what gonna be happened to women study? He doesn't believe women has to be educated.

Kajoli (Bangladesh)

It was really a difficult time for me. I used to go to school when I was six years old. So I went in the school for four years, yes, and after that I hate that school and the teachers because it was really difficult time for me.

I got difficulties at learning. And if I did any something wrong, they just take the stick and punch me! You know what I mean? Like, if I didn't do my homework, or if I did any noise, or if he asked me any question and I didn't answer, or if I didn't know the answer: he used to did that.

So I was hating the school. I doesn't want to go anymore. And after that I stopped to go to school. I was about ten.

Mostafa (North Africa)

I wanted to go to school but they don't take me to school. I was living with my aunts. They take their own children to school and leave me to the house to do the housework.

I don't know how to read and write. I just know how to write my name. And I practised how to write it.

In my country there'll be a lot of people there speak English. I tried to learn English before. When I came here, it's very hard for me to talk to people and I struggled a lot before I speak this English.

Haddy

My parents are peasant farmers. So I had to work in my parent's farm field since when I was very young, since when I was like seven to be precise. I used to help my parents with the farming, and looking after herds at the same time.

Unlike my parents who did not have any opportunity of study, I studied up to undergraduate education in my home country. And in August of 2010 I graduated with a bachelor's degree in geography from the Eritrean Institute of Technology.

Yusef (Eritrea)

All I need is just the school to help me because I have a learning difficulties, so all I was just need was help. But, nobody cares there.

Other children were treated same like me. Anybody don't know the answer? If he doesn't know anything? Same thing happen [corporal punishment]. If you complain? They doesn't care, because they think this is the best way to learn. And when he do this, he just do this to scare you to learn and to get you to learn the things. But this is not true. If he did this, it's gonna get difficult for you, but there is a way if he just tell you the best and shows you a little a bit, this the good things.

Better than doing the sticks.

Mostafa

I always went to the morning classes. And in the afternoon, I would go to my family's farm field and work there. That's how it is.

We used to have animals: goats, cattles, donkeys, camels. We had lots of animal when I was very young.

Yusef

After I left the school, my father told me, "If you didn't go back to school it's not good. It's better for you to go back and to learn the thing. I think will be good for you in the future."

So after that, I hate the school. I don't want to go back again because of these things. So I told them, I'm not going to go back.

He said, "If you don't go back, you're going to get to work, doing jobs and these things."

I said, okay, I like to work. I don't want to go back to school.

He said okay. He talk with somebody and he just take me to work with him. So I started working. So after a month he asked me, "The best way is to go to school because the work is really hard for you and the good thing is to go back to school."

I said don't want to go back. I like to work, and the work is really good. And it was really difficult for me of course, because I was like eleven years old. So I tell them I like to work and I'm not gonna go back.

He said, "Okay, up to you, I don't mind."

So yeah, I keep working, working. And after that, I just had a problem with some peoples…. And lots of things happened…

My job was to prepare the walls before painting. We used cement and sand mixed with water. The cement bag is really heavy, it's fifty kilos. It was really painful and tiring because it's hot as well. We work from the morning till the evening. My father was just trying to do this to get me back to school. He just wanted to get me tired because he wants me to learn and to get a good future. I didn't enjoy the work but I said to him I like it, because I didn't want to go back to school.

Mostafa

You see, my father he doesn't like to put us in a government school. So he put us in a private school from KG1 [kindergarten]. And at that time, when you are in a private school, you are going to take much care from the teachers; not like the government. And of course I'm so happy to go to the school. My father would take us by the car and drop us. We have to wear the uniform and it is a nice feeling that you go, but when you find yourself they give you too much homework, you don't like the school! But we get used to it. My mother and my father they're helping us in teaching us, and sometimes we are taking private lessons just to improve our degree in the school

June (North Africa)

I didn't get, like, the opportunity to be supported by my parents in terms of the academic side or the intellectual side of the education, because my parents were uneducated. So I had to educate myself, working with my teachers, classmates, in that environment.

The school environment was so important for me. But it was a little bit different from the home environment where I didn't have any support for the education-related material. So all my support for educational stuff comes from the school environment.

Yusef

Usually we don't have a mixed school: the boy alone and the girls alone. So, sometimes, the boys in their school they have to come and tease us, the girls, when we are in the coming to the school. When you think of your childhood you remember for something like that.

June

Back in the village, I started learning A–B–C–D. And then we learn our own language, because that's very important for us. And in the refugee camp, it was still very basic.

When I applied for a scholarship, I had to write essays in English and fill the application form in English, and do an interview in English. It was a big, big struggle for me. But I tried so hard, because I wanted to get this scholarship. I knew that this was the only way to get me to education and to study at university. And the first time I wasn't successful, but I was very lucky the second time because I got it. Many, many young people wanted to get this scholarship, and, among thousands of students, I was selected.

I remember when I was in Bangkok, I had attended a special English course, as part of the university course. And after the class, in late afternoon, when other students were going back home or going to other places, me and my friends, we had to go to the computer room and started typing A–B–C–D. And it was a struggle for me to look– where is A? Where is B?

And that happens for a year. And then the second year, I find it easier. And the third year, I was okay with the course.

Mima

I have a long hair, so they don't believe that it is real. They thought it is artificial. So anyone pass through me, they have to pull my hair and I shout. Which is not good from all the time. Even my brothers they get used to do that! They pull me from my hair and drag me from the bed down to the floor. Which is make my eyes, I have bleeding, at my eyes, which has become so red, bleeding. Half of my eyes it was red! So my mother and father they took me to the hospital, they give us drops, and my mother she told them that usually the boys do that to her. So they stopped them doing that to me. Naughty boys, sorry!

June

In the area where I come from, we have lots of beautiful mountains and trees and flowers and rivers. In some areas the mountains are very high and we have beautiful waterfalls.

Where you have the lake besides the mountain, the air was so fresh and nice.

I remember it was very difficult for me to climb to the mountains because we had no other means of transportation. So we walked through the jungle, climbing very high mountain for two days. And when you reached on top of the mountain, and when the breeze came in, it was so wonderful! So natural and beautiful! And it made me so fresh and relaxed.

Mima

The city where I was born is a Ghulja city, it borders with Kazakhstan. So the region itself, the Chinese called Xinjiang Uygur Autonomous Region, and we prefer to call East Turkistan.

So the Uygur region or the East Turkistan is about six times as big as the UK. It's the second largest desert, Taklamakan Desert, in the south, and the North is very much mountains and hills. And so I come from the area where is grassland and heavenly mountains. From the distance, you see the snow peaks, so it's a very, very beautiful, beautiful region.

Reyhan (East Turkistan - China)

My dad was a very hardworking man. He also had political ambitions.

I remember he was a very busy man, but one thing I can remember when I was a young boy is that we were always looking forward to Saturdays. Because Saturday is when dad would come home and we would all get into the car and we would drive around and we would drink sodas. I mean, we were so crazy about Fantas! I mean maybe it is nothing to people who do not know the concept. But as a young man, we were always looking forward to going out to drink Fantas and just to drive around and see the countryside. And it was so wonderful. It was so fantastic.

So that is the memory I have of my dad: we are always looking forward to Saturday when he would be home and we would go around, drive around talk, he would show us things, and it was a very happy moment when I was growing up as a very young boy.

And these are the memories that I have of my dad.

Idris

We don't have pets in the house.

Something happened to my cousin's daughter: a dog bite her and she died. The dog got rabies. So that's why I was scared of dog. I can't cope with dog and cat. Cats as well. Because in my country we don't take the dog to the hospital and stuff. We don't keep the dog and put chain on the dog to walk around. They always leave the dog going around. They going around, around, in the street. Sometimes the dog is come from the forest and going round the city.

And she go out and the dog bite her. That's why she died. It's very sad.

The child got rabies as well. They don't give her water to drink. They give her nothing. They said if they give water its going to shout like a dog. She got rabies so they don't allow her to drink. That's why her mum cry. She always said, "My daughter die without drink water." Very sad.

Haddy

Growing up was not fun, because I grew up in the village and we didn't have all the social amenities. I remember that sometimes we used to go hungry.

When I was in high school I was one of the best students in my school but I did not perform. Even when I was going to sit for my final exams in school, I was not in school, because I was at home, because there was no money to pay the school fees.

So that is the context under which I grew up. It was not fun. Sometimes I used to be sent home for not paying school fees. And then when I get home, I could find that my mother did not even have enough food to eat. Because again, we were many- we were eight in the family. And at that particular time, we were actually four in high school, and it was only my mum, and she was working as a teacher. And the money was not enough.

It was not fun. It was not fun.

When I became a journalist, it was not very difficult for me to take sides. It was very obvious to me how to take sides. Why? Because I was brought up in poverty. I was born and brought up in the village. I was educated in the village. I only came to Nairobi when I joined college. So I used to see things in black and white. Either you are with me, or you are against me. So it was not very difficult for me to take sides when I was a journalist.

And the reason why I became a journalist first and foremost is that I was seeing the things that were going on as I was growing up. And I used to admire certain people because they were so fearless in locking horns with the state. And that is when I started to recognise the power of the pen. And I was like: when I grow up, I want to be like so and so, because they had the power of the pen, even though the government had the guns and all the powers and authorities that they had. But these people who I consider to be my role models had just the pen, and the pen was doing wonderful things. And that's what made me decide to become a journalist in the first place.

Idris

I'm fifteen years old and I'm Kurdish. I was nine years old when the war started in Syria. At first, it was far away. It was just kind of away from us, but we were included at the same time. I was that kind of girl that was just trying to be away from everything that's happening. My mum and all of my mum's family were trying to just make me stay away from the politics and everything, because that's how dangerous it was for me. As a young girl, it was really dangerous and threatening for me to talk anything about politics in public or outside my house. Especially because I was Kurdish as well. Some of you might not know about it, but Kurdistan has been struggling with trying to gain an identity and build their own country. So being Kurdish it was an even more dangerous thing for me to talk about the President or talk about the war.

Yezda (Kurdistan- Syria)

They used to call me the rude boy!

I remember when I was in Nairobi. And of course, I was a crime reporter by then. The PC (Provincial Commissioner) was a man called Francis. He was a very tough man. And I used to report about the security situation in Nairobi and its environs, and I didn't have nice thing to say. I just used to write the way I see it.

So, one day, I go to the news conference and then this man, Francis, was very livid because he had taken us to a peace meeting but, instead of reporting what he wanted us to report, I really reported on things that I thought, in my view, were more newsworthy than just to take a script written by somebody to go and re-duplicate it and then put it on the paper. So I wrote my own. And the following day, when he called on us for conference, and I was there, I think I was the only one who wrote unflattering things about the peace meeting. And he was very furious.

He said, "There is a man called here Idris- every time I do good things, he's always writing rubbish about me! There is somebody here called Idris, who is this?"

So he was very livid. And then everybody in the room started laughing, because they knew who Idris was. Of course, the man knew the name, but he didn't know the face. And everybody in the room knew me, but nobody was going to say who Idris was! But that is the context under which I was I was working, the man was very livid. But it was also comical, in a way.

Idris

Birthday party we don't do. Nobody like my parents do these things. We can celebrate for Eid and weddings. Of course they do some weddings. I remember I used to go there. It was quite nice. They just dance with some music. Lots of people come and say congratulations, and if in the man house you go and say congratulations. The man house is making some food for the people who comes, so you can have some food. But in the girl side they don't do. If he's rich, then he can get a flat for his wife; but if he's okay, they can live in the same house as his parents. He have to pay her family before she get to his house. Something called *mahr* [dowry]. So you're giving this money, the stuff she need to get it, for her parents. But she doesn't give anything like that to his parents. She just gets some stuffs like clothes, thing for the kitchens. But the man has to get everything, like the flat.

If I have a girlfriend what am I going to do? I have to get married first. Not like here!

In my country, if a guy like a girl they can have sex, but if this thing happen the guy gonna leave the girl because it's really, really big problem in our society. If this happen maybe they can kill the girl; if she have sex with anybody without marriage, if her family find out she has sex with somebody else before marriage.

Of course the man get in trouble as well. He get killed. Not maybe. If they find him and they know this person who did this to the girl, they're going to kill both of them, or if nobody doesn't know anything about this, then they can get them married. But if the people know, they have to kill them. Because they're going to talk about you, they're going to say something about you. They don't want people talking about them … They want people to think about them they're really nice people … and all these things.

Mostafa

Early years- Notes

There is no such thing as a refugee. Not really. "Refugees" only exist in the eyes of the host population. Each individual is just that- an individual. They might be mothers, doctors, students, journalists, and so on, but there is no shared identity possessed by all refugees.

Refugees are far more marked by their difference to each other than their similarity, in terms of religion, language, culture, ethnicity, gender, sexuality, politics etc. Refugees are the least homogenous group imaginable. It is important to situate their accounts in the personal, so that our respondents are not merely being asked to re-enact their "refugee story"- the same story that they were forced to give the Home Office to secure their sanctuary. It is what the refugee writer, Dina Nayeri, calls the hagiographic journey, a story of escape and salvation that she was forced to retell again and again to earn her place in society, an endless act of prostration that she came to resent. By grounding our journey in the early years, with all of their trivialities and tragedies, we hope to avoid flattening everyone out to fit a uniform narrative.

One thing that jumps out about the early years of each respondent is the division of class. Some of the speakers talk about private schools and privilege, whilst others talk of battling just to access school at all. Class plays an important role later, in determining how far people can move geographically, as well as how well they might resolve certain barriers. As our respondent, Idris, explains: "You cannot be mobile unless you have resources."

Another significant topic is that of people's parents- either as agents of inspiration or of damage, and in this we see the universal in the human condition.

Trouble with the authorities

I used to go to those gatherings which was in the streets. But after some time, the regime started to attack these kinds of gatherings- which was open, which was public- and they attacked us and beat us. And, in one of the places that I was going, once a boy of fourteen was shot, and he died.

So, when these kinds of public gatherings couldn't take place, we went underground.

Yasmin (Iran)

I started as a reporter. And, as a reporter, I used to report on certain things. And I was asking myself: how is this possible that our government, that's supposed to protect his own people, can do these kinds of things?

Idris

I took part in mandatory military-training and open-ended national service which contributed to my decision to flee the country, Eritrea.

I was taken to Sawa, a military training camp, when I was only sixteen, to undertake intensive military training and participate in the matriculation exam for grade twelve students. I then went on to complete a bachelor's degree at the Eritrean Institute of Technology, as I say. After that, I was recruited into the indefinite national-service where I had no control over my day-to-day activities. I tried to speak up and resist the violent structures set up by the government, but it wasn't safe for me. So I had to leave Eritrea.

That's why I started by calling Eritrea a "carceral state".

Open-ended national service, arbitrary detention and forced disappearance, coupled with the country's isolation and sanctions at the international level make the condition of life in Eritrea worse for every citizen. These explain why the country has been haemorrhaging its youthful population for four decades.

Yusef

I had to leave my job. Because every time I was coming home from work, especially if it was late: I was interrogated. You know, they had barriers between some places, and when we were going out of Tehran, or coming back, they would come up to the buses and ask people to come out. Not everyone. They would choose people. And even they would stop taxis. They would get you in the street asking you, "Where are you going? Where you come from?" Lots of questions.

Yasmin

And I got deeper into this, because again, I was now seeing the injustices that was happening. And I was like, no, no, no, no, no, no, this is something that I have to take a stand on.

Idris

Once I remember, I was in a taxi. It was late. And they stopped the taxi and asked me to go out. And they interrogated me and they searched my bag. And when they asked me to go out, they asked the taxi driver to leave.

And I thought that the taxi will go because there were other passengers. And I was very worried they might arrest me. And even if they don't arrest me, how can I go home now?

Yasmin

I was under political surveillance. So it would take me one hour to get home, something that I can do in twenty minutes, because I used many, many, many different means to get home. Like: you get off here, you get off there, you get to another bus, you get off.

So that's how we used to move around. Because I was under political surveillance and people were following me.

And sometimes I used to talk on the phone, and I know people are listening.

Idris

After the revolution and the struggle for independence, the government came about in a perfect condition to behave in the way they wanted to behave. There were not any checks and balances, there were not any institutions, nothing in Eritrea. It was for the government to build a new system of governing the country and taking it forward. And that's where they failed from my own perception.

There were a lot of other challenges as well, like the border war with Ethiopia, which happened when Eritrea was in the process of like creating laws and drafting its constitution. And then when the border war started, the whole thing was completely suspended forever, for indefinite time. And that has made Eritrea to become a completely self-colonising state, where it became a lawless state. And that's what I call it a carceral state.

Yusef

The good thing about being a crime reporter is that you cannot become a good crime reporter unless you have contacts. And the good news is that I had contacts within the police. And of course, when I had to talk with the police, I was also advised the best place to hide is within the police unit itself. I had a cousin who was a policeman. So I was living within the police quarters, yet I was being hunted by the police.

Idris

It's the failure of the government to recognise the challenges that they would face after they become independent. They were revolutionary fighters. They know nothing but the war and fighting and trying to remove the colonial powers.

But the colonisation has totally changed the social-economic organisation of the people in the country. It was a subtler type of colonisation during the Italian time where people were put in hierarchies that they have never known before. People were not allowed to even move or walk across the street and live in the villages that they used to live in, where their ancestors were born. So it's completely changed.

It was kind of a chaotic situation for the government to come and start a new way of organising the society. And, it may be small, but things like the family as a unit of social organisation were completely broken. Even after independence, because people are completely disintegrated in the country, where some family members are in the national service for an indefinite time, some other are in an arbitrary detention, and some other people are leaving the country.

So the family itself as a unit of social organising doesn't exist in Eritrea, and many people feel homeless in their own homes for that reason.

Yusef

My professor told me [that I would get in trouble]. He said, "With your temperament? Three things. Either you're going to end up in jail for a very long time. Or you're going to end up in the grave. Or you are going to go into exile. You cannot escape these three things with your temperament."

Idris

Some people are involuntarily immobilised in the country because they are unable to move. Maybe they're put in detention centre, maybe they are stopped at a checkpoint. It is not easy to escape.

But some of the people who have the resources to escape, or the desperate people who are around the border areas, can try to escape the country. They are trying to leave the country for their own safety. It isn't for economic reasons, or for some other reason, it's people fleeing to save their lives, to stay alive and to survive. And that's what they are denied of in the country for most of their lifetime.

Yusef

It is the joy of a journalist: you do all your investigations, maybe for months, and then you write a report and you lift up the phone and call the concerned Member of Parliament. "Alright, sir, I have this story. This is the introduction, please. What is your comment?" I mean, that's the most fantastic part of doing a very long report.

And then they're like, "No, no, no, no, your report is not complete, come and talk to me."

And then you got there and they stall and stall and stall, until the time for going to press comes, and then they want to bribe you or something like that. But to cut a long story short, this is what characterises the work of a journalist. It's always very dangerous.

And sometimes a journalist is called in this manner, and when you get there they have already set a trap and they trap you: somebody puts something in your hand and then they arrest you for extorting money, or they damage your reputation completely.

So these are some of the ways that the powers that be use to discredit and sometimes to arrest and incarcerate journalists. They frame you with obtaining money by false pretence, or by trespassing, whatever it is that they can put on you at particular time is what you go down for. So it is a very dangerous thing sometimes to report on these things.

And of course it is true. Because there is a drama that I did in the Parliament House where the MPs meet. And it also made my case a little bit notorious because this is a news story that I had worked on where I was being bribed [to suppress the story]. It was the first time I saw a real money bribe. And of course, I thought I was being entrapped and then I would be arrested. So I threw the money up in the air. I just made a drama. And everybody was in shock in the room. And then that is when they said, "The rude boy with nothing! The rude boy with nothing. He is proud but doesn't have anything."

But again, I didn't reject the bribe because it was morally reprehensible for me to do that, it was simply because I panicked. I thought I was being entrapped. So it was just like my survival instincts kicking into place. So that's why I did it.

And at that particular event, my own uncle was in the room, and he saw what happened. So they used to call me the rude boy without anything.

I would rather be the rude boy with nothing but I have my integrity intact. Because I grew up as an orphan and I saw what happens to us. And my mum used to tell us, "My son, let me never hear that people, especially the rich people, and the powerful people use you to oppress the poor. Shame be upon you if you do such a thing. And the curse will always be upon you."

So these are some of the words that I used to think about. And the injustices that I grew up seeing is actually what made me to see things in a black or white. But, of course, I've outgrown that simplistic way of seeing things.

Idris

My problem is that I claim here as an asylum seeker, but my asylum seeker is just been refusing so many times. So, you know, I'm so feared to go home because of that government is still there.

So even if they say today that they will send me back home, I'm just feared to say I don't think I will come out from the airport. They will hand me to the [secret police]. And the [secret police], I don't know what they can do to me. So I have got a problem. So I'm just stressing.

Rose (Southern Africa)

Women's Bengali culture is not used to having pets. We badly treat on pet, but people in our country who are rich, they have a dog and they're well looked after. But my time is there is no pets. But we had a connection with the wild crow in our family. My mum used to put them out some food. So all these we used to.

I realised our Asian women life are in a cage. And so, in my performance art piece, I want to do like bird in a cage, and in that performance I want to make them free. So that was my concept.

When I went to buy the bird in a shop and shopkeeper knows, I told them, I'm gonna let them free to go. And shopkeeper says they don't want to sell their bird because you've made them free and they're tamed. They're not going to be survive outside. They're tamed already. So the symbol of the cage is about the question: is it tamed by human power?

So Asian women is same.

Kajoli

In 2009, they started this sophisticated camera system, installing in all the corners, especially targeting the Uyghur neighbourhood. They installed the maximum cameras to make sure that everything is seen, people's movement, including the mosque, who is coming in, who's coming out.

They gradually made it into a police state. So now we know that every two hundred metres there are checkpoints for Uyghurs. All Uyghur households have the barcode. Uyghur's ID card is linked to its own DNA, bio data. In 2016, all Uyghur people, including other Turkic Muslims, received notice from the government that they must go to hospitals and give blood.

So everyone was summoned to hospital and they must give blood, five cubic millilitres of blood samples. And they must give a voice sample, so you'll have to read one paragraph of written notice twenty times; they record you twenty times.

And the facial recognition: so they are taking photo from all directions, including taking photo of your iris. In the room where you go in, they have very big equipment, very advanced. People are told to remove their clothes, naked, and stand inside. And that takes photo of all directions.

That is all taken and installed in a database with the fingerprints of every Uyghur.

So the state has everything about what is their blood types, their DNA.

Also, you must have heard about this notorious business of organ harvesting? So, that [the DNA database] made it very convenient for the Chinese government, when they need an organ, it's very easy for them just to look and check, whose blood samples match the people who needs organ.

So it's terrifying situation. It's… it's absolutely terrifying.

Reyhan

Despite not being able to return to my home since 2000, I kept a very close contact with all my sisters and brothers. I call them at least once a week, speak to them, and telling them about my music, anything not sensitive. And also they want to know my son who left when he was seven years old. So, you know, they always fascinated about life in UK and they really look up to me. All of them have very simple, simple life, and they very content with what they have.

And then in the end of 2016, suddenly, I couldn't get hold of anyone.

Calling the landline, calling the mobile, even my sister's children, my brother's children, even the grandchildren, some of them I had a telephone number. I couldn't get hold of anyone. No one would answer my phone.

And then even in the New Year, I thought- it's the New Year, they must answer my phone call. And I actually already knew something really, really bad must be happening.

In the beginning, I thought oh, is that because someone died in the family and they feel uneasy to break the news or whatever? But then later, I just thought something is happening and they might lockdown the region, something is happening.

And then on the third of January, I just called my brother non-stop. I thought I won't stop until they pick up the phone, because his phone was ringing all the time.

And eventually he picked up the phone. It was very sad. Terrible.

Normally, every time when I called it's always like a joy, you know, the other side they just like lit up, "Hey, how you doing?" But he was very kind of silent, as if I'm a stranger.

I said, "Why no one is answering my phone calls?"

He said, "They did the right thing."

He was very, very quiet. The sound was just heartbreaking. I didn't know how to respond. And I knew it was as if he was being watched when he when he was speaking to me. And then he just said, "Leave us in God's hands."

Reyhan

Trouble with the authorities- Notes

Successive UK governments have postured around populist vote-snatching rhetoric on reducing immigration by removing the "pull factors" that draw people to the UK. Back in 1995, Michael Howard stated that, "We must be a haven, not a honey pot," before stripping 13,000 asylum seekers and their families of the right to benefits and accommodation. When she was Home Secretary, Theresa 'Fields of Wheat' May, outlined a raft of policies to introduce what she called a hostile environment, in order to deter illegal immigration. The hostile environment is a sinister phrase borrowed from the lexicon of pest-control, where it is used to describe the denial of food/water to creatures such as rats and cockroaches, and is thus a reincarnation of the dehumanising metaphors of genocide and ethnic cleansing.

But asylum seekers are a statistically insignificant percentage of the total number of immigrants to the UK, so these policies are more about saving money and looking tough than about actually controlling net migration. Asylum seekers are not motivated by the allure of benefits or healthcare. As our respondent, John, explains: "All these things called 'benefits' here- I don't know anything about it and I don't want it. I want to work and provide for my family and provide for this nation."

Asylum seekers are not pulled to the UK. They are pushed to leave their home countries.

In this chapter we start to build up a picture of the push-factors: the real reasons why any of this is happening. We see the impacts of living under repressive dictatorships and autocratic regimes where the military deathsquads and the secret police have unchecked power, and where journalism is suppressed.

And we start to build up a picture of the kinds of people who would dare to stick their head up and take action to resist. Not cockroaches and rats, but democratic champions and everyday heroes.

If the UK government really wanted to ensure that nobody claimed asylum anymore, then the most useful way would be to ensure that nobody had to claim asylum anymore, by promoting human rights through diplomacy, aid and trade to tackle the problem at the root cause: the push-factors in the country of origin.

Arrest

One day when I went to see a friend, but he was arrested already. He was tortured and he gave up our meeting point to his interrogator. So I was arrested.

Yasmin

I remember many journalists have been arrested. When I was working, there was a time that my editor and one of the senior reporters had to be arrested because they would not recant a story. So this is a tale that was going on for quite some time.

Idris

I was a spokesman of the student union and I was equally the leader of the university human-rights club. I endured a lot of persecution, ranging from arbitrary arrest, detention, torture, and imprisonment. Throughout my years in the university, I was arrested in three different instances, detained by the gendarmes, the police, the secret service, and the agents of La Republic where I underwent severe torture.

John (Cameroon)

Sometimes it happens such that nobody knows that you are arrested. Like the time that I spent most in jail in Kenya, nobody knew I was arrested. I only talk to my uncle who would not do anything because he was in the military. So he could not do anything because of his military background. So he didn't do anything. But to cut a long story short, that's the longest that I sat in jail; nobody knew I was in jail. Even my editor didn't know that I was arrested because, when I was arrested, it was not told to anybody. So then what happens is that you're taken from this police station to another one, to another one, to another one, but such that nobody can actually find out where you are.

And then the funny thing also again, this is the tactic that the police was using: when they want to disappear you, your arrest is not recorded in the occurrence book. So you go to a particular police station, alright- so-and-so was arrested, he was brought here, but there is nothing in the occurrence book. So if any of you would want to make follow up, you have nothing to go from, because you go to the first station of instance, where you probably know the person was taken to, but he is not there, he has already been transferred. He was here, here, right. He was taken to police station B. When you get there, he's not there, he's already been transferred.

So this is what actually what happened to me.

Idris

I took part in a peaceful protest denouncing the government's poor human rights record. Since I was a leader of the human-rights club at the university, I equally did champion this cause. I was targeted and detained when I was arrested for four months at the Kondengui, a highly secured prison for political dissidents.

John

Well, of course, we know that some people are sometimes seriously harmed. Some people are disappeared. We know people who have disappeared without a trace.

Some people are arrested, and then you never hear about them again, and then maybe they are found in a forest somewhere there, or they are dismembered and then you find many, many parts in many, many locations.

So these are some of the things that happened.

Of course, it is also not a secret that the Kenya Security Service had a death squad within their rounds. And of course, one of their own came out and confessed, because he was part of this squad that was executing people. And, of course, he was also murdered in a similar manner.

So these are some things that are out in the open. It's not like my story, but it is out in the open.

Idris

I thought I was absolutely harmless. I was not dangerous or anything. I was basically taking pictures. I was just like, seventeen. I didn't imagine that they would think of me as any kind of, you know, risk or sort of threat that you would want to lock me up for that. I thought even if something happens, even if by any chance something happens, they would just realise I'm just a little kid or something. Maybe I don't know, slap me or something? Just give me a kick and let me go. When they see my ID they will see I'm only seventeen. They'll think oh, he's obviously not a terrorist or a foreign spy or whatever, but just some stupid kid.

When they arrested me they took my ID and broke it in half. And when they delivered me to the police station, they didn't know that I was a minor because I didn't have any ID to prove it. And I got sentenced to fifteen years just like the adults.

Ali (Egypt)

To tell you the truth, if and when I was being taken to court, I didn't know what I was being charged with!

And when I was produced before a judge and the charges were being read, I was in shock! And it was not like I was being charged alone- I was now brought in with a very big group. And I was now part of that group. And it is one charge and then everybody has to yell, "Yes."

Whether you are silent or whether you yell, "No," nobody cares, because your guilt is built by acclamation.

And again this is the Mungiki group [banned ethnic organisation]. Now, everybody else there, I'm not saying that they were all guilty, but, of course, there are some of them who actually have confessed that they belong to that particular group. And some of them are just found in the wrong place at the wrong time. And then they are arrested in that manner. And then they are put in one group, and then they are herded into court. So that's what happened to me.

Idris

Arrest- Notes

Arrest is the pivotal moment when your former life is over, and things will never go back to the way they were ever again.

Not all of our respondents have been arrested, of course. Many left their country before coming to the attention of the authorities. But those who were arrested are speaking not just for themselves but for all the other people who do not have a voice of their own, either because they are still in prison or because they have been "disappeared"- secretly executed and disposed of by a government deathsquad.

Trust is a huge issue when you are working with refugees and asylum seekers, especially when you are in what appears to be some official capacity such as an immigration lawyer or casework advisor. And it is no wonder when people come from such totalising regimes, where every aspect of life is controlled by the government and everything gets back to them eventually. When we have been undertaking casework at Refugee Radio, we have struggled to convince people that even the electricity and gas companies are not part of an elaborate state apparatus. Asylum seekers are left afraid to complain about any institution or agency in case it somehow gets back to the Home Office and harms their case. Even once they have refugee status, this fear lingers. Most of our respondents were too scared to go on record saying anything bad about their experiences with the NHS or the JobCentre or anyone else because, every time they open their mouths to speak, they feel that sudden hand on their shoulder all over again.

Prison

The Joint Committee Interrogation Centre was full. There were so many prisoners that they used the corridor. Actually, I have a painting about that.

I was in the corridor for a month.

I was blindfolded the whole time. Imagine! Twenty four hours a day we had to be with blindfold. So, yeah, it was full. And some prisoners died under torture. Some prisoners committed suicide after being under torture for so long that they couldn't take it anymore. So they committed suicide.

Some of them were saved and put under torture again.

Yasmin

I was arrested on October 2013. I spent six years and three months in prison. It was just like this really crazy experience. And then I got released, and I've been out of prison for almost two years now. And it's a lot quicker to say that than it was to live through it!

Ali

I was there for six months. My parents were going to different prisons asking if I was there, and they're told that I'm not there.

Yasmin

Throughout my childhood I've been known to be this, you know, perfectionist nerd, always fretting over getting an A instead of an A+ and stuff. I was this person who always liked things to go according to plan, so much that everything was planned like five years in advance. So obviously prison was completely out of plan, and it just destroyed everything.

The first couple of months in prison, it was just torture for me. For me, this was kind of a shock. I just couldn't comprehend it. And I spent maybe the entire first year in prison, just uncomprehending, like: I'm in prison? It would come and hit me, you know, every now and then, like: I'm in prison. I'm in prison. After I got released, people keep asking me, "Are you like fully aware now that you're outside of prison for six years?" And I tell them I'm not I'm not even fully aware that I was in prison in the first place.

Ali

The prisoners used to talk a bit during, for example, the night, or something like that. But I remember the first week of my arrest, because of the beating, I was so tired that I was asleep day and night. And I couldn't believe it. I mean… I woke up sometimes and I heard something, some prisoners whispered something to each other, and I went back to sleep. It was, I don't know… it was unbelievable.

Yasmin

Sometimes, of course, you become mad.

But again, you go to prison, and you think you are the one who is hurting. And then you go in there and then you find the people who are there and you start to hear stories. I mean, you just are struck by the injustices that are happening. Like somebody has been in prison for a very long time, or somebody has been in remand prison for more than, let's say, five years, and there is nothing that is happening. When you hear their circumstances, you find, all right: I've just graduated to another level. You just find out that you have a tale to tell.

And the best thing that you can do is to encourage people and say to them, "Alright, we are here, we have to make the best out of it. But when I get out of here, I will make these stories known."

But again, it is always a painful situation for me… What shocked me most when I went to jail was the first day, because on the first day I was beaten senseless. Not by the prison wardens or anything, but these ones they used to call them like the prisoner in charge, like the big man in prison, the prisoner who is in charge, they used to call them the "trustee".

So one of them hit me. I don't know why he didn't like me, but he hit me seriously. And that was the first time that I cried my heart out in jail. I was hurting: one because I was accused of things that I didn't do. And I knew that it could not be proven. And then number two: nobody knew where I was, not even my mother knew where I was. So I was hurting at that particular time, but what hurt me most was the thought that I was being beaten and I was going through all this out of something that somebody was putting on me.

Idris

When I talk with people about what the most torturing thing was in prison for me, it was this idea of not having anything under control; not even if you're in a particular cell, you could be like moved to another prison the following day. You don't know.

The following second upon hour, you just have no idea whether you'll be spending the night here, whether the people you're spending your time with will be here tomorrow; in a minute, they could be moved as well. Someone could be released, someone could be arrested and then moved into your cell. You could be in a cell of five people, tomorrow's fifteen, another day it could be a packed cell of sixty people, then you're just in solitary confinement. Sometimes you have books, sometimes everything, and then you get a search and they take everything from you. You just suddenly don't have anything but the clothes you're wearing.

So it's just this whole thing is it's really hard to adapt to, when I'm someone was always trying to control my circumstances and how I operate in life.

I had to somehow adapt and adjust to this new status quo of nothing under control at all. Nothing, not the people surrounding me, not where I sleep, not the people who come and go outside my life. Not when I see my family, when I don't see my family, how long I see them for, not what I read, what I write, what I get access to, what I don't. So yeah, it was really, really hard.

Ali

The guards were doing their job. They were harsh. They believed in the regime. And because the regime was saying it's a state of God, you know. And they believe it. They loved Khomeini and some of them would die for him. So they hated us. Because they believed the regime hated us.

Yasmin

Athazagoraphobia is the fear of being forgotten.

I was sentenced to fifteen years so I used to write on the wall as a therapeutic process. I had the wall behind me, and I turned it into some sort of gallery of quotes of music or just kind of random drawings. I suck at drawing, so I just kind of scribble on the wall, write what I think of, write my feelings.

Sometimes I would stick pictures to it of my family members, maybe friends. It all had to do with kind of letting everything out somehow, and sort of grounding myself, to remember that these people were my family, these were my friends; because I was starting to forget. It gets a bit fuzzy with the years. Especially that you don't see your friends anymore and no one's allowed to visit you.

So, in time, you sort of start to doubt that you were ever outside one day. You keep thinking like: was I born in prison? It starts to get hazy, like the memories are more like dreams. You know these dreams when we wake up and we can't recall them very well? It started to happen the same way, maybe after four years, and by the sixth year it was really, really getting bad.

And then people obviously as well forget you. No matter how loyal friends are, they move on, they graduate, they get married, they have kids, they have jobs, they go on with their lives. And the people who used to send you maybe letters every visit, start to kind of lengthen into every month, then every couple of months, then every year and then nothing at all. They just started dropping like flies as the years passed. And then by the sixth year, there was basically no-one asking and no-one sending letters. So it was this kind of mix of you forgetting everything outside and everyone outside forgetting you as well. This was athazagoraphobia, this fear of being forgotten and forgetting everything.

So I wrote on the wall as a document to ground yourself and remind yourself that okay, I was out there, I did have those friends one day, even if no one asks about me right now. They were there. I was there. I was in between them. And I liked to put pictures of myself in between the photos of my friends, just to kind of see this, to keep this mental image of me with people who were not prisoners, who were not just in this context of prison and prison suits and guards and stuff.

Ali

I knew I was sentenced to execution because my friends were executed.

I was transferred to Evin prison which is where we were going to have our trial. The court just took one or two minutes and the judge asked me just a few questions.

The final question was, "Would you confess to wrongdoing?" And, "Would you say you're Muslim?" Things like that?

I said no.

And he said, "Okay, go."

And I knew that it meant the sentence will be execution.

Yasmin

In prison they separate the criminal prisoners from the political prisoners. They're just like, kind of segregating us from each other. And, actually, it's funny, because they're more worried about the prisoners with the criminal backgrounds, that the political prisoners could somehow kind of radicalise them or idealise them or talk to them about politics. So from the start, we were kept away from any kinds of prisoners.

And we were put in separate cells. They treated us worse at the start. And then sometimes it was better in terms of treatment. It all depends on the general situation of the country, how the country is doing. Like if the direction is okay, then kind of lay off them a bit now, don't hurt them, just like leave them be, and then then political prisoners will get treated alright, no-one tortures them or anything. But then if there is one incident of something going on in the country, then it just switches. They start the confiscations, and they take everything we have, they can beat us they can they can make life hell for us. Or they can give us a break. It all depends.

Ali

I wasn't the only one. And we all die one day. I didn't want to do something that I regret later. So I try to live my life in prison.

Can I say something? It wasn't only that time, that I was waiting for my execution. Later on, a few years later in 1988, thousands of prisoners were executed. They first stopped our visits with our family and then we heard that they have started to kill male prisoners. Then one day they started to interrogate us, the female prisoners. And one day they took more than fifty women from the prison I was in. And they never come back.

Later on we heard they all were executed.

Yasmin

"Took nothing, saw nothing, know nothing," it's the criminal prisoner code.

One of my really good criminal friends was like, this huge drug dealer who used to trade weapons. He was the head of a gang. And it was just a crazy experience for me. For some reason, we became friends. He wanted one day to send a message to his mother on the outside. And no one trusted him. They were scared of him and no one wanted their family to interact with anything regarding him. So I just agreed to deliver the message. And he was really touched by the whole gesture, because political prisoners sometimes tend to kind of worry about making their families contact anyone on the outside. So when I did this, my mother called his mother and delivered the message to her, he was really grateful and just didn't believe it. And then he started warming up to me, speaking to me, and then we used to meet up in the recess, exchanging stories and stuff. And yeah, he just introduced me to this whole world of the criminal underworld in Egypt and the dealings with the authorities, how to sell drugs, how his gang was run. He used to tell me like stories and experiences of how one half of his gang would steal and kidnap people and then the other half used to do the Robin Hood thing of bringing things back to people and getting money or fees in exchange for it. So it's basically operating in two ways.

I got to know a lot of more prisoners with the same background to him. So it's fascinating. I don't know what kind of personality or not I've experienced that I would have never had access to without prison, obviously. So it's just a whole new world for me that opened up of people from the extreme left to the extreme right, different ideologies, and then people who are drug dealers and murderers and stuff like that. So it was fascinating. It was scary at times, but mostly fascinating.

Ali

After I was released, my sister took me to a hairdresser. She touched my hair and said, "Ugh! What are you washing your hair with?"

And my sister told her, "She just came out of prison."

And the hairdresser was shocked. She was just shocked. And she said, "Oh, sorry."

Yasmin

Parents are arrested to tell the regime about their children's whereabouts.

And I remember a mother who was tortured and she used to tell us that she was scared that she wouldn't bear the torture and that she would tell them the address that her sons were hiding. And one day after she came from the torture, which was bastinado [flogging the soles of the feet], she committed suicide and she died.

There were lots of hostages back then, but it was this kind of hostage.

We had a woman. She was my friend. She was she wasn't political at all. She was arrested because they wanted her brother. They told her, if her brother comes and turns himself in, they would let her go. Or that she should tell them where her brother is. And these people knew if the loved ones get arrested, they will be executed. So they stayed in prison and told their families to tell them not to turn themselves in. So they stayed in prison.

Ali

Whenever I was going out, the regime's agents started following me. Very openly. I don't know if they realised I was active again. I don't know. But, at some point, they started following me.

It was very difficult to escape, so I had to be careful not to go to a friend's house who were not my friends from prison, you know? Because it was natural that my prison friends, we saw each other, it was normal. But the other people had to be very careful.

First, I thought it's only that I'm imagining it. But I did some things like, when I was passing the window of a shop, I stopped and, looking at the goods, I used to try to see if that person who was following me in the other street is still is coming, and pass me again, and what is he doing? And I realised, yeah, I was being followed.

But then a time came when they realise I don't care anymore. They came to my face, showed me that they are following me. For example, I once wanted to make sure he was following me so I went to shop. It was grocery. And the man who was following me came to the shop, picked up a potato, a big potato, and asked me, "Is it good?"

I said its fine. Then I said to him, "Fuck off."

Sorry, I shouldn't say this!

Yasmin

These camps [in Xinjiang] are concentration camps. The mass arrest started in April 2017. We know there are people who were released and the state of their mind or what happened to them just completely destroyed them, mentally and physically.

And we also heard that for a lot of young women, after being released, the suicide rate is very high.

Not only the forced sterilisation, but mass rape is common.

Prison- Notes

There is prison and then there is prison.

We might make distinctions between jail and prison, between a custody suite and a young offender's institution and a secure unit. But then there are Ghost Houses. A prison is a place where they have a written record of the prisoners, where there is at least some connection with the courts and where some kind of justice is at least seen to be done. A Ghost House does not work like that.

The term originated in Sudan, but there are Ghost Houses around the world. They are remote buildings maintained by the military, the secret police or other shadowy agencies for the clandestine torture and execution of anyone who has come to their attention. This is not to say that those things cannot, or do not, happen in a regular prison, but in a normal prison your fate is less assured. In the Ghost House, your fate is absolutely certain, even if nobody else will ever know what happened to you.

The state apparatus is so brazen in some countries that their versions of the Ghost House are not even secret. And some of them are vast.

Insein Prison in Burma holds ten thousand political prisoners. It was built for half that number. Some of the cells hold as many as a hundred people in one room, and conditions are so crowded that prisoners are actually paying for floorspace to sleep on. Prisoners have been subject to beatings, torture, and mass executions.

Sednaya is a military prison in Syria that is notorious for torture and executions. Human rights groups put the death-toll somewhere between 5,000 and 30,000 detainees in the last ten years.

In Iran they have made a museum out of the old Anti-sabotage Joint Committee (Towhid Prison), to show how bad things were under the old regime, whilst the new regime simultaneously runs ongoing facilities such as Evin Prison (population 15,000), where political prisoners are subject to rape and torture. Evin Prison even includes a special yard just for executions.

People such as the Uyghurs are also imprisoned in concentration camps, as our respondent, Reyhan, explains in this chapter. These are euphemistically branded as "re-education camps," but their true purpose goes far beyond simply detention or punishment.

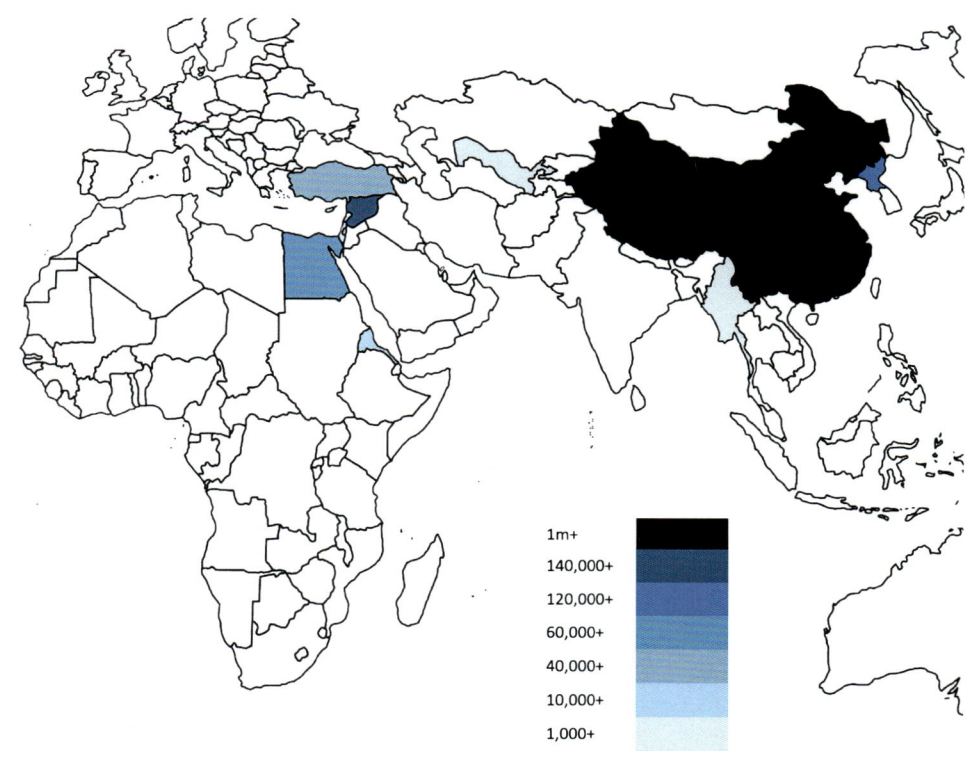

Number of political prisoners by country, 2021

Country	Number of political prisoners
China	1,001,598
Syria	149,862
North Korea	120,000
Egypt	65,000
Turkey	40,000
Eritrea	10,000
Burma	7,013
Israel/Palestine	4,650
Uzbekistan	2,000
Bahrain	1,400

(Source: Congressional-Executive Commission on China, Syrian Network for Human Rights, U.S. State Department human rights report, Committee for Human Rights in North Korea, Arabic Network for Human Rights Information, Stiftung Wissenschaft und Politik, Amnesty International, Addameer Prisoner Support and Human Rights Association, US Commission on International Religious Freedom etc, compiled by Kong Tsung-gan, 2021).

These figures are only estimates, as there are few official records of political prisoners. In Syria and China for example, the government denies that it has any. The figure given for China in the chart includes the 1,598 identified by the United States' Congressional-Executive Commission on China (CECC) as well as the 1,000,000 Uyghurs and other Turkic minorities who are detained in the Xinjiang camps for "political re-education." Official Chinese records from the Xinjiang High People's Procuratorate record 540,826 prosecutions in the region in the past few years. Given a 99.9% conviction rate this would mean 540,285 people formally imprisoned, but Foreign Policy magazine and other sources put the real figure in the camps at closer to 1.8m.

Torture

I was arrested in the street. I was not taken to a police station. I was taken to a Joint Committee Interrogation Centre, which was in the hands of Islamic Guards Court. They used *bastinado,* which involves hitting the sole of the feet. And they beat me until I was paralysed.

And it wasn't all. Two times they gave me electric shocks here, behind my head, to force me to accept the confession, which I didn't. And at some point they bashed my head to the wall which caused a tumour to grow and made me epileptic.

Yasmin

Well, they have very many ways of persuading you. Some of it is the torture or you can be just put in in jail. You are just left there; you don't know what's going to happen.

Idris

While in detention, I was subjected to degrading and inhumane treatment.

I was stripped naked and tortured. I was kicked and punched many times. I was given electric shock. I was asked to sleep on a cemented cold floor littered with water. I was raped several times by the secret agent. Sometimes I find it very hard to talk about, particularly this instance, but I have to say it, because I want people to understand the ordeal that I've been through because of my views and because of my commitment towards the cause of the Anglophone Cameroonians.

The conditions in their cells were despicable and very awful. No electricity. And I was not given any access to medical treatment, despite the severe physical injuries I did sustain during my torture.

I and other activists were tortured with impunity by the secret police force. I was frequently beaten with iron rods, rubbed in mud, kicked from left to right. I was asked to stand in a pool of water for a very long time. And it was very hurting. I was only given food once a day. And one thing that you must remember in Cameroon is that there is a gross abuse of human rights while in detention. The conditions they are despicable, are horrible. The fact that we don't have a bed, you sleep on a cemented floor, and it's all littered with water. We don't have any toilet. We have to use a bucket and we all defecate into it and it stinks all night long.

I was finally released with others by the intervention of the president of the Cameroon Human

Rights Commission, the late Dr Solomon Nfor Gwei. And I remember a very nasty situation when he came to intervene on our behalf to be released, it was very appalling that he himself was detained. He was arrested. And they said that if he cares, let him call the president and tell him. That was president Paul Biya, whom we know has been in power now for the past thirty years. It was a shock to so many of us because we couldn't believe that in somebody in such a position could be arrested by a secret agent.

John

I think that the biggest torture, especially, I have to endure- is the waiting and not knowing. The waiting and not knowing.

Like, you know have gone to prison, but you don't know when you are going to be produced in court, maybe your file is lost somewhere, somebody disappeared your file. So you are in a limbo, you don't know when you will appear in court, and you don't know how your case is going to end.

So it's a very difficult moment for some people.

And, of course, it's one of the greatest torture that an inmate can have: the indefinite wait, and not even knowing what the charges are.

Idris

Torture- Notes

Many of the refugees and asylum seekers we support at Refugee Radio are victims of torture.

Torture is ostensibly used to get people to tell you things that they want to keep secret, but it has never been a reliable tool: most people will just tell you whatever it is they think you want to hear so that you will stop torturing them. So, torture is always used with secondary purposes in mind- to punish people, to scare their allies, to instil fear in the population, and, perhaps darkest of all, to satiate the cruelty of the torturer.

Torture damages people permanently, both physically and psychologically. The repercussions of torture can have effects on individuals and families that ripple out into the world internationally and intergenerationally.

In a sense, it is ghoulish to talk about torture and to share the stories of torture that we have heard at Refugee Radio, but to keep silent about the matter does a disservice to the survivors and rewards the perpetrators with a secrecy that they do not deserve.

It takes a lot of courage for people to be able to share their experiences of torture, even when they are making their asylum claim and could be relying upon it as evidence of their persecution. But not even then are you guaranteed that anyone will listen.

A Sri Lankan man claimed asylum in the UK a few years ago. He was a member of the Tamil ethnic minority group. He told the Home Office that he used to melt gold for the Tamil Tiger rebels before he was captured and detained by the army. The army tortured him because they wanted to find out where the gold was hidden. The man had to provide details about everything for his asylum claim– how the soldiers heated up metal rods so that they were sizzling and then held them down on his arms until the pain made him pass out. Then, while he was unconscious, the soldiers pressed the burning rods into his back. This left him with deep scars over his body.

His case was refused because the Home Office did not believe him. He took it to appeal and in 2019 the Upper Tribunal made the astonishing decision that he had inflicted the burns himself in order to support a false asylum claim. They called the wounds "self-inflicted by proxy".

How did they come to this conclusion? To begin with, they had to ignore the evidence provided by the medical expert brought in to advise on the case, Dr Zapata–Bravo. They also had to ignore the Istanbul

Protocol (the official United Nations' Manual on Effective Investigation and Documentation of Torture and Other Cruel, Inhuman or Degrading Treatment or Punishment). They also had to ignore how unlikely it would be for someone to deliberately cause themselves such deep injuries on the off-chance it boosted a future asylum claim, not to mention the fact that evidence of self-inflicted torture wounds for asylum claims are basically non-existent. Then they had to ignore the fact that the wounds on his back could only have been administered by a second person while he was unconscious, which meant that they then had to ignore how difficult it would be to find someone who had the medical training to administer the anaesthetic needed, but who lacked the medical ethics that would stop most doctors from contemplating such a thing.

Then they had to ignore the widespread evidence of torture by state forces in Sri Lanka. Thousands of Tamils have been detained for as long as five or even ten years without charge. In 2020, the Human Rights Commission of Sri Lanka found that 84% of the Tamil prisoners detained under the Prevention of Terrorism Act were tortured after arrest. The European parliament recently declared that the act "breaches human rights, democracy and the rule of law".

But the Home Office somehow found it easier to ignore all of that in favour of their bizarre "self-inflicted by proxy" theory.

It's no wonder that people do not rush to speak out about torture. I was cross-examined once at an immigration tribunal hearing about a torture-victim's asylum claim. The Home Office lawyer asked me why the claimant didn't disclose his torture immediately upon arrival in the UK. I replied that he was too traumatised. The lawyer then asked me why the claimant talked about it in an interview on the Refugee Radio show after his asylum claim was refused. So they don't believe you if you don't disclose it, but then they also don't believe you if you do.

You can't win.

War

Since '93, the Western governments, especially America and UK, invaded some countries, like Afghanistan, Iraq, Syria, and other countries. And so it's inevitable that there will be refugees from these countries. I mean, we have people who escaped from these countries that the Western governments made a mess of.

I mean, they killed them, bombed them, ruined their house and now they don't want them here. What a logic!

Yasmin

I was sitting and doing my school homework. And suddenly, there was mortar bomb landed and the crackle of gunfire. And everyone had to run for their life. My mother was calling out our names. "Little daughter, little daughter," she called on me and she said, "Run! We all have to run."

She said we've been attacked. I was frozen in fear. I didn't know what to do. But then I knew it was very important for us to escape because I knew how women and villagers, they were used as slaves. The women were gang-raped by the Burmese army soldiers, things like that. And we ended up in refugee camp again, after a long time walking in the jungle. And my mother suffered from heart failure but we didn't have any medicine or nurse or medical treatment.

Mima

It was the 31st of May when ISIS started to attack us and started to come to our city. We woke up at 4am in the morning. All of my family were woken up by the voice of a bomb next to us. It was five meters away from our house. So we woke up and we just didn't know what to do. We didn't know what was happening. We thought it was so horrible that we thought ISIS are in our house now. That's how scary it was for us.

Me and my little brother didn't know what's going on. So we just had my mum telling us, "Just go back to sleep, it's nothing, I think it's the voice of the television, the volume was up. So there, is nothing much there."

So we just try to convince ourselves: yeah, it's nothing, it's just the television. So I took my little brother, he's two years younger than me, I took him and just told him, "Okay, let's just sleep, and we'll see, everything's gonna be alright, in the morning." We couldn't sleep at all, because that's how much horrible it was.

Yezda

I crossed the border illegally back into Burma with politicians and journalists and campaigners. And I met a woman who was forced by the Burmese army troops to carry heavy loads, and to carry military supplies for the region. She was gang-raped by the Burmese army soldiers. And when it came to the time, her father defended her. The Burmese army soldiers were shooting her father, and her father was killed.

I also met a family who were hiding in the jungle in a camp. And he was explaining to me how the Burmese army fired mortar bombs in a school building, injuring two children, and then killed one boy. And this family they were very lucky to have escaped. And they told me how difficult their life was to escape this attack and survive.

Mima

We had our suitcases and all the things that we had to take, like: two trousers, two T-shirts and stuff that we needed, just in case we actually have to run away. And this moment did come that we just had to run away, because ISIS were really close to actually come and get us because in my house, we were mainly girls. It was me, my mum, my aunty, my grandmother. And the only men were my little brother and my granddad. So for us girls... and I'm sure that you do know how the ISIS treat girls...

It was so threatening for us. So we just wanted to leave the house.

Yezda

I met a boy who escaped from the Burmese army. He was forcibly recruited as a child soldier while on his way to visit his grandmother.

In Burma, there are about seventy thousand child soldiers, and many of them were forced to join the army. And they were given choices like, you have to go to jail or you go to join the army. And children, they don't want to go to jail. So they joined the army. And they were not given proper military training, but they were sent to different area to kill, to burn down, to destroy houses, to rape women, to commit many kinds of human rights violations.

Mima

So, no one happy to leave his country, but we were out of control- a lot of war, a lot of like bad situations.

Every day the children die, woman, man. It's hard if you need to dream for some simple things in your life or to make your life better, just like safe place. We couldn't feel safe in our country and so that's why we left our country and we was looking for a safe place, to find safe place for like to be easy for you to sleep, and to feel comfortable, to be healthy, to be looking for everything good for yourself, or for your life, or for your family. So that's why we leave our country.

Saleh (Middle East)

Living in a refugee camp was very difficult at first, because we didn't have any identity card or passport. And we were put in a small camp. It was more like a prison camp. We were asked by the authorities to fence ourselves with barbed wire. And we got very basic supplies.

We were not allowed to go out from the camp. We were not allowed to travel into town or anywhere. And although we had basic food, supplies, medical supplies and educational supplies, life was very difficult. The Burmese army and their troops still attacked us inside refugee camp. So we were not happy at all in refugee camp. We continue living in constant fear.

Mima

I was 15 years when my dad retired, and we moved back to Damascus. And what happened to me as a teenager, thirsty to discover my roots, and my own heritage, walking down the streets of old Damascus, is one godly experience. The architecture yells out loud. "Look at me!"

You walk these streets, and you not only notice Islamic and biblical architecture, but you might be walking among Roman architecture, Greek architecture, or Umayyad architecture; there are layers and layers and layers of different civilizations that have come and gone in one place. And rightfully so, you are walking through the oldest continuously inhabited city in the world. This is not my saying- this is the United Nations World Heritage Site. And to me, living and questioning what is going on socio-politically, that architecture was the proof to me that we are a diverse group of people.

Because if a certain religion was as bloody as it's been portrayed out there, not a single church or synagogue would be left standing in Damascus or Aleppo.

So to me to be walking in the 2000's, witnessing the millennia-old architecture, side by side with merchants, with kids playing, with pigeons flying, it was the mirror proof, the screaming proof, that this society is coexistent and a very diverse one.

Why is that super important today? Because Syrian refugees are being portrayed as, well, you know, I don't need to tell you how they're portrayed…. You can just open the media and see what how Islam or Middle East or Syrians are being portrayed.

So why is it so important to re-own our own narrative and to say, look at our architecture? Because these extremist groups are not even a fraction of societies and they're not even older than twenty years. Right? Most.

Look at my city. Look at a church right next to a mosque that coexisted for fourteen hundred years.

How is it possible that animosity has always been there since between these groups? How is it possible that this architecture does not have a single dent in it? Tell me: I am an architect, I am begging you! How is it still pristine? The evidence is outstandingly loud. And that's why I fell in love with it.

And it's super important to keep reminding people of that story.

Mo (Syria)

War- Notes

One of the most common themes from our respondents on this topic is the use of sexual violence as a weapon of war.

According to an Amnesty International report, rape has been used as a deliberate and organised military strategy, especially in inter-ethnic conflicts such as Bosnia, Darfur and Rwanda where it was a tool of ethnic cleansing. This leads to the fragmentation of communities and rising rates of HIV infection. But in the post-war period, women do not receive the support they need because the problem is dismissed as a personal crime against individual women, rather than a strategic warcrime. Being identified as a victim of rape can damage a survivor' status in the community, and the stigma prevents collective action.

"Women survivors face emotional torment, psychological damage, physical injuries, disease, social ostracism and many other consequences that can devastate their lives [...] The violence women suffer in conflict is an extreme manifestation of the discrimination and abuse women face in peacetime, and the unequal power relations between men and women in most societies" (Lives Blown Apart, Amnesty International, 2004).

Persecution on the basis of sexuality

I grew up in a very Christian home. My parents were very, very churchy and we pray every morning and night, every afternoon, always praying.

Basically, I went to Catholic boarding school, where we were taught that homosexuality was completely abnormal and we were taught that it was more like satanic views. When anybody did something like that, you were considered evil. So let me say, from a very tender age, I really didn't understand what it was all about.

Until when I was about fifteen in college, and I had a female friend, she was kind of younger than me, and we're always together. I discovered that I have a feeling for her, but I knew this was wrong because it was taught as abnormal. This is the devil's work, you understand? It was like, no, you can think about that but I always find myself attracted to her. We always want to spend time together, we want to cuddle, we want to be together. But it just always looked wrong, according to what we were told.

So we always used to try to hide it but it was rather unfortunate that one of our seniors in school saw us one day, and she reported us to the dormitory mistress. The mistress called us in and it's just like, "What were you doing? How could you do this? You know what this is?"

And we were like, "No, we weren't doing anything, we were joking, it was just jokes and everything. We're sorry. We'll never do it again."

We apologised and she punished us for two days.

So literally, that's when I actually had an enlightening of what this was- being lesbian, because I actually realised I felt more comfortable around the same sex and I had feelings, certain attractions.

At that time, I didn't even know what the legal parameters were. I think I wasn't that exposed to that. But what I knew was the Christian views on that, the church views on that, I knew that. But I didn't know the legal implications. I just knew it was something which the whole society did not accept. No one would want to hear about it. No one want to hear at all about it. But I didn't know the legal penalties until I was a little more older, when I was going to uni. By that time, I knew exactly what were the penalties, because I had witnessed the case of a guy who was caught and he was beaten in public. He was almost killed.

We had the police come there, dragging him through the doors to the station. And it was... it was really cruel. Like, you can't even fit into the society because people always marginalise you and just treat you really bad.

Even among friends, if you had maybe a guy who started behaving funny, like, a bit feminine or something, you had other guys gang up and plan and beat the person up, you know, all the sort of stuff. It's hell. It's traumatising. You don't want to through that.

Patience (Cameroon)

I came in this country not as a refugee. I came here to do my studies. But I was born a gay man.

When I was living in Uganda, I have no problem with it, because we know we have to keep it separate to live in Uganda if you're a gay man. I managed that. So when I joined the college here in the UK, I had a friend that I used to live with back home as a gay man. He got attacked. He was not killed, he survived, but he changed the city where he used to live. I called him and he said to me, "Oh, it looks like I got found out. Now they know I am gay." I said to myself, okay, if they know that, then they also know about me. Then I made a choice not to go back.

August (Uganda)

My mum, she knew. Because I called my female friend, and talked to her and my mum overheard my conversation. And that's when she found out.

She just thought to herself that she should pray about it and it's going to go away. So she always used to pray about it like, "I know she's gonna get out of this. This is not normal. This is going to end because if this doesn't end, my daughter's life is ruined."

That was what she had in her head so she would always pray against it, but she knew. She knew that being lesbian is never going to help me in Cameroon, and I'm just gonna end up being killed or locked up for years and everything is just gonna go wrong.

Patience

When they do the marriage, I didn't go. I didn't even know they do it. They don't even ask me. They don't even ask me or informed me.

I wake up one day and my mum told me they do the marriage in the mosque. And I was crying because I don't like that man, because I hate him. I asked them why did you do this to me? They don't take my permission, they don't say anything to me. I was crying the whole day, the whole night, because I don't want to marry him.

After I get married I get my first child with rape. It was my cousin who raped me. When they do the marriage, they don't tell me. Because in Muslim they always go to the mosque and do the marriage. If you there or not.

Haddy

The most easiest thing is death, because you will be beaten up by an angry crowd, beaten to death. So even if you are lucky enough to go to prison, you will be put under torture and your chances of surviving are very little. So either way you're still going to die.

Gabriel (Central Africa)

It got to my parents, it got to church, it got to the society. The whole area where I grew up in found out, and I got texts from my friends telling me: what's going on? What's happening? Oh, my God it's everywhere! What happened? Is it a joke? Is it a false story?

At the very beginning I had to start denying everything and saying it's a lie and everything, but it got to the point where I just told myself, if he's not going to forgive me, if my life is really threatened back home, why am I going to carry on lying?

Patience

I was caught in a hotel with a partner due to a text message that I sent to him. Unfortunately, his brother went through his phone. He saw the text message and he followed us, so they caught us at the hotel.

That evening we were badly beaten up by an angry crowd. Luckily the manager of the hotel called for the police to come in and take us. The police came and rescued us from the angry crowd. But later on they took us to the police station where we were stripped naked, our feet were tied up and our heads are facing down. They tortured us; put our heads in buckets of water. Beating, kicking was what they did all the night, then later on they pour cold water on us and ask us to run on concrete. And after all the beatings, one of the officers kicked my left arm and twisted it. So, because of the fracture that I had, they stopped beating me and they took me to the hospital, where I was there for three days. Then later on, discharged. When I was discharged, I knew I'm not coming back. Because I was supposed to go back to the police to sign up, waiting for the date I'll have to go to court. But when I successfully left that place that day, I knew I am not coming back.

Gabriel

My mum tried to call my dad and ask him if he was going to come to my graduation but it was like, he's not going anywhere. He doesn't know me. He disowned me. If he sees me anywhere around Cameroon with the girl he hears I'm with, or without, I should rest assured he's gonna kill us both.

My mum was crying. She was like, "How would you say that? That's your daughter."

My father said, "Oh, no, that's your daughter. That's not mine."

Patience

My girlfriend, my partner at the time, she knew what was happening and she was like, "This is so unfair. You know what? We're gonna do this, I'm gonna get married to you, so you could actually stay here legally and live your life and get your job," because she knows how focused I am, and she's like, "You had a distinction in your master's and I know you have a lot planned. You have no future back home. You have no life back home. I'm gonna get married to you and then you can stay here."

I was like, "Are you sure?"

She was like, "Yeah."

I was like, "Okay."

We decided that's what was gonna happen and everything was okay. That was at the end of December. My visa had to run out in January. So, December, everything was ready. And I'll never forget, on the 15th of January, I was supposed to go to London to start the preparations for booking a registry and everything, and I get a call from her. She's like, "Oh, can I talk?" She said she wanted to call me on Skype. She calls me on Skype and she's crying.

I'm like, "Why are you crying?"

She's like, oh, she's so sorry she has to do this to me.

I'm sorry, I'm saying this and I'm getting a bit emotional, because it was the worst day of my life.

She told me her family can't accept her to marry

someone who's not Nigerian, because she is Nigerian, and she was born here [in the UK]. So she was like, her family won't accept it and she can't do it for me.

I was like, "Where do you leave me now? What am I supposed to do now? What do I do?"

She was like, she was sorry, she can't really help me again.

I was just… I was lost. I was like, "Do you want to get into another relationship? Are you seeing someone else, or what's going on?"

She was just like, "I'm sorry, we can't be together, I'm so sorry." She was crying. And she hung up.

My life went to pause. A standstill. I couldn't think. I called my mum and I told her, "I'm coming back. I'm gonna come back. I'm gonna get killed. I'm gonna die. I don't really care. I don't think I have any life anymore. I don't have a shot at being happy in anything. I'm just going to go away. I'm coming back and I don't want to hear anything. And if they're gonna kill me from the airport? Fine. That's it. There's nothing."

She was crying on the phone with me. And it was a total disaster.

Patience

Claiming asylum as an LGBT person is a lot more involved. You have to prove that you are gay, which is very, very difficult to prove to anyone. When I applied for the first time, they asked me, do you have a partner? I said them, I don't have a partner. And they said, "Okay, so that means you are not gay." That is the system!

I had to tell my solicitor this time (because last time I didn't know), to get my country information to the Home Office so they will know how a gay man or an LGBT person can survive in Uganda.

Because from your date of birth you know yourself you are gay, and you know in this society it's not allowed. So from the start, you start learning how you going to live your life in society.

It is very difficult to prove your case as a gay man in this system. As much as everyone say, "Oh, it's legal now, you can live as a gay." Okay, but in this community still you get picked on. Sitting on the bus as a black man, I still have my black friends that I live around and I associate with a lot: when I'm around, you can still see their faces, they're like, "He's there." It's like what it's all about? Yeah, I'm here. But because of the system they can't do anything to you, that makes you a bit more comfortable.

But back home, it's not like that. Once someone say, "He's there", maybe could be your last day.

August

Persecution on the basis of sexuality- Notes

There are five categories that may be used to claim refugee status, as outlined by the 1951 Convention relating to the Status of Refugees and the 1967 Protocol relating to the Status of Refugees:

1. Race
2. Religion
3. Nationality
4. Political opinion
5. Membership of a particular social group

A successful asylum applicant will need to convince the Home Office that they belong to one of these categories and that they risk persecution in their country of origin specifically because of that category.

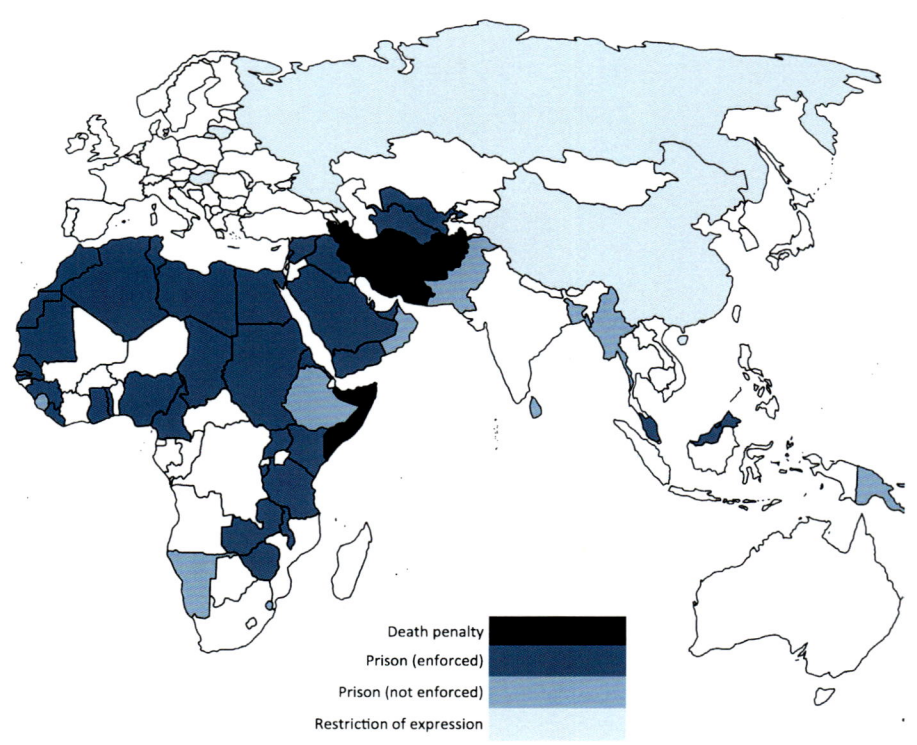

Worldwide LGBTQ laws, 2021

Sexuality was not originally considered to constitute a "social group," but precedents established by case-law over the last twenty or so years mean that it can now be included. Up until 2010, the Home Office would try to argue that the applicant should go back home and live covertly, keeping their sexuality secret and relocating to a new part of their country if needed. But then two cases reached the Supreme Court- one involving a homosexual man from Cameroon and the other from Iran. In Cameroon, you can be sentenced to between five and twenty years in prison for homosexuality, and in Iran you can be sentenced to death. The Home Office had successfully argued in the Court of Appeal that it would be "reasonably tolerable" for both men to hide their sexual orientation to avoid further persecution, but the Supreme Court ruled that, "to compel a homosexual person to pretend that their sexuality does not exist, or that the behaviour by which it manifests itself can be suppressed, is to deny the fundamental right to be who he or she is."

Flight

The time came for me to run after some of my colleagues had been murdered. One of them was gunned down in the streets.

I received a phone call. This was a policeman, he was in Intelligence. When I was in the media, I used to have quite some money. And when he was going to wed, I was actually the best man in his wedding, the guest of honour, so he respected me because I gave a lot of money in his wedding. And he respected me generally. And he told me, "No, no, dude, we have your photo. So please, run."

And of course, for somebody to tell me that, I knew I was in danger.

He told me like, "You saw what happened to your friend?"

I did.

"Yeah, run. We have your photo."

And of course, when a policeman tells you that they have your mugshot, it means that you have been marked, so I knew I had to run. And of course, the first place to hide was within the police barracks, and then, after that, I didn't have any money, because at that time my accounts were frozen. I didn't have anything and nobody who wants to help me had anything. So it was actually my mum who had to go to the bank to borrow money. She borrowed a thousand dollars. And that's what she gave me. And that's how I ran away.

I ran away.

Idris

The YPJ [Women's Protection Units] are kind of like a smaller group of Kurdish people that were trying to help people to run away from the city. They helped us and they managed to get us away, to kind of run away from the city. I remember that I was actually crying because I didn't really want to leave my friends, and because my family was still there, two of my uncles didn't really want to leave, and my grandad as well. So I was really crying. I was really upset because I didn't want to leave my city at all.

Yezda

It's called a "Bastard Run."

You run, you don't know where you're going, you don't know how it's going to end up. But you just know that you have to get out.

And mama told me… this is what my mama told me- when she was coming to get me out of prison for the last time, she was like, "Son, promise me that this is the last time I'm going I'm coming to get you out of out of either jail or prison."

And I was like, "I can't promise you that, mum. It is just like telling a cock to stop crowing in the morning. When the morning comes, the clock in the cock's brain just make it to crow. So I cannot promise you that."

And then she was like, "No, son, if that's the way it is, then I'm either going to bury you, or you have to run. You have to get out of this country."

Idris

So we really didn't want to leave Syria, because it was everything that we had. We were really proud of being Syrians. And it was really good. We had a really great life there. But we just came to a point that it's dangerous for us to even stay at home because we were so scared. We were thinking of what if some day would come and we actually wouldn't have a roof, or we didn't have anything to actually live in and we might just die in the street. So it was at that point that we just had to go. We didn't want to. We had to leave Syria. And we actually did.

Yezda

Like I was telling you- I was in a Bastard Run.

I had been kicked out of Uganda. So in Uganda I was a persona-non-grata. And actually I was to be arrested on sight if in any case I arrived in Uganda. So even my journey through Uganda was a very funny one because I had to pretend to be somebody I was not. I pretended to be a herder on a truck full of goats and cows and all manner of things to make it to Sudan.

Of course, in Africa, there are porous borders. You can sneak across the border without anybody noticing.

Idris

The UK and Europe and Australia were kind of a dream for me, because when I watched TV I was like, "Oh my god, mum, imagine me going there when I grow up, because how sick would that be?" But I got to the point when I had opportunity to leave my country and I just didn't want to. Before that, I didn't realise that I really liked my country that much. But we just had to leave.

We went to Iraq, and we lived there for one year. There was a UN programme so we went and applied there. We had a couple of interviews there. And they could give us a way to run away and come to UK. They made the choice to actually come to the UK: we really didn't mind; we just wanted a house that we can feel safe in. They told us that UK would be a really good country for you, especially that it was just me, my mum and my little brother. Especially for us, it would just be such a great future for us. And we were really happy about it. Like I told my brother: "You remember when we used to dream that we go to the UK? Well, now we have the opportunity." So yeah, we actually got on a plane and we just came here we found ourselves in the UK, the time went so quick, that I remember it was like it was yesterday, when I was running away from my house in Syria.

Yezda

The first thing that you need to do is to move. And you don't move without funds. If we find that you don't have money, you don't have finances, or your accounts are frozen, or something like that, or your petition has already been completely damaged, so nobody can trust you. And in that particular sense, the thing that you can have the best solution is always to have a protection fund to make you move. Even if you have to move across the border or you have to be smuggled, it costs money.

So there is a coalition of human-rights defenders that I work with very closely and anytime that a defender is in trouble and they asked me what do I do? I say right: mobility. I cannot move without money right? Call so and so. Do this, do this. So this is basically what I do since I came out here.

I have to say this: when a human-rights defender gets on the run, or the moment, you realise that your life is in danger and that you have to run away, the first line of defence is always mobility.

And you cannot be mobile unless you have resources.

So that is what I realised when I had to run, and it is actually what made me come up with a coalition of organisations that give individual human-rights defenders protection funds so that when they are in danger, they can move.

Without mobility, you are already dead where you are.

Idris

So people should understand that these refugees and immigrants did come from an established life at the end of the day.

It's not only "off the boat", but what happened before life came crashing down all of a sudden, that's also as important to be told.

Mo

I came to UK because I wasn't safe in my country for me.

Daryan (Middle East)

Part Two: Living in Limbo

"I met people who have been stuck in the asylum system for ten years without any documentation or legal status. When I asked them what it is like to be an asylum seeker in the UK, they told me that it's like living in Hell. Some others describe it as living in a grave- in a state of incompleteness. That tells you how cruel this hostile environment is."

Yusef

Living in Limbo- Notes

Limbo is a region of the afterlife on the borders of Hell, similar to the Asphodel Meadows in Greek Mythology where people were consigned to eternity if they were too bad for Heaven but too good for the abyss. As a metaphor for the asylum system, it could hardly be more apposite.

You are not allowed to work while your asylum claim is being processed. The government says that people would journey to the UK and make fake claims just to access the labour market by the backdoor. It is not clear how much of a problem this would actually cause, if at all, but preventing people from working certainly causes huge problems. First, it creates the foundation of what is effectively economic segregation, an asylum-apartheid that continues to exclude people from accessing services and opportunities even after they get status. Second, it infantilises and de-skills people, robbing them of their professional identity when they should be working to establish a new life for themselves. Third, it wrecks mental health, compelling people to a depressing and anxious period of uncertainty and inactivity. And, last, it costs a bomb.

There are currently over 60,000 people who are still waiting for an initial decision on their asylum claims in the UK. This is the highest it has been in a decade. Of these, 75% have been waiting for more than six months. And of these, 75% have been waiting for more than a year. Thousands of people have even been waiting more than three years. It costs around £9,000 to accommodate and support someone for a year while they wait for their decision. According to a recent Refugee Council report (Living in Limbo, 2021), the total cost per year of the backlog of people awaiting an initial decision for more than six months is estimated to be approximately £220 million. And this is taxpayer's money that is being spent to stop people from working, people who would otherwise be contributing to the economy and paying taxes themselves.

The Home Office has always run with a huge backlog of cases. They have never employed enough caseworkers to deal with the number of claims they receive. There is no political willpower to do anything about it, and the situation has become an unofficial aspect of the hostile environment i.e., anything that makes asylum seekers suffer is considered to be a good thing. The Coalition government announced a target for making initial decisions within a set period of time back in 2014, but the Home Office quickly abandoned this and there is now no target whatsoever and no published service standards.

Journey to the UK

Every refugee who has left his country, or her country, it's not easy to arrive to the safe country. About me: like my journey take about two years to arrive to the UK and a lot of… a lot of bad things happen in my journey.

Saleh

The UK doesn't want refugees.

That's why they try to not let them in. Especially the boat-refugees and asylum seekers trying to enter the UK on boats. They turn them round. Pushing back to the sea. Doesn't matter if they die, if thousands die.

And I wonder what's the difference between shooting people or hanging them, like what the Iranian government does? What's the difference with turning the boats and pushing them back to the sea and let them die? Killing them. The UK government is responsible for thousands of deaths in the Mediterranean Sea.

Yasmin

Most Eritreans stay within the neighbouring countries. There are thousands of Eritreans in Sudan, and in the capital city in Ethiopia. There are also many other Eritreans in the refugee camps in in those places. And that has been the case for generations, particularly for Eritreans who became refugees before the country's independence because of the colonial occupation. They're still refugees in places like Sudan, or Ethiopia. And that has been the case.

A few of them, the people who have resources and the physical capacity to come to places like Europe, including the UK and other places, can come to the UK, and that itself is a risky journey. It's a life and death journey through the Mediterranean Sea, through the Sahara Desert, and that in itself is regulated by human traffickers. So it is very risky. And many thousands of Eritreans die in these lifeless deserts or in these treacherous waters.

Yusef

My immigration case took me nine years.

I was frustrated. My mental health went downhill. And I felt like I was treated inhumanly, if that is a word. I didn't feel like I was human during that period.

During that nine years, I was just being stripped of my humanity and I couldn't do anything: I couldn't go to see my mum when she was unwell; I couldn't go to pay my last respect to my two brothers when they died; I could not work; I could not study; I could not do anything!

So I was just existing. Barely, barely existing. I have no focus in life... It messes with my mental health because I feel like I don't have any purpose.

Oba (West Africa)

When I arrived in England I feel comfortable to be safe and the police told me, "You are safe, don't be scared, you are in a safe country."

Daryan

Journey to the UK- Notes

This is a short chapter.
One of our clients at Refugee Radio was being assessed by mental health services recently and they asked him if he crossed the channel on a dinghy. He didn't want to talk about it so they asked us instead. We didn't know. They were shocked when we told them. The fact is that we had deliberately never asked.

There is an ellipsis in Saleh's quote at the start of this chapter- he says, "A lot of... a lot of bad things happen in my journey." Hidden inside that ellipsis is two years' worth of suffering and trauma that he just cannot talk about. It would be a cruelty to ask him to relive it just for the details, and we didn't need to know, so we didn't ask.

We spoke to a refugee youth worker in our previous book (Castaway Heritage 2019) who was able to talk about some of the things his clients had experienced in their journeys, and some of the stories were heartbreaking:

"I remember two young girls from Eritrea. They were actually kept as sex slaves in Libya for an extended period of time and I think by the time one arrived in the UK she was pregnant. She didn't know who the father was.

"Then another one is of a family. This was actually a family from Eritrea. One, the dad was separated in the trucks that were driving them across the Sahara Desert. The females were put in to one truck; the males into another truck. The traffickers, without letting anybody know, just drove the female truck in one direction and the male truck to Libya. This gentleman, I don't think he knows where his wife and son are, up to now. So it might be they have been sold into sex trafficking as well in Egypt, or Libya, whichever it is. So the journey can be horrible in itself.

"Another one, from Afghanistan, he was shoved in a car boot for an extended period of time, driving through Iran. I think the way he was sitting, the truck in the boot most probably had an impact on his knee, so since he's been in the UK, his knee has been messed up. He has to have surgery and everything. It most probably is dislocated because you are sat in the same position for a long time, so the journey can add to the trauma people experience."

It is difficult for people to talk about their experiences with traffickers and people-smugglers. Some of them work for global criminal organisations who are still active in the person's country of origin and who can threaten family members who have remained behind. In other cases, they can still have an impact on the individual's life while they are in the UK, so it can be dangerous to speak out.

In the emergency UASC (Unaccompanied Asylum-Seeking Children) hotels in Brighton, there is a rotating population of recently-arrived young people aged 16-18, mostly fresh off the boats from Calais. They have been retelling their stories in comic book form, which makes it easier to confront difficult experiences and remain anonymous. Again, we didn't ask them about their journey- but the stories were just pouring out of them. In almost all of the comics that involve crossing the channel with traffickers, there is a panel at some point where their lives are threatened with a knife or a gun, often at the point of boarding an unseaworthy dinghy on a French beach.

Detention

Yeah, we come to the safe country, but also we lose our mental health.

Saleh

When I arrived in this country, I was told that UNHCR will be at the airport, basically, all you guys will be at the airport waiting for me and opening your arms. And I was expecting flags of the UN.

It wasn't like that. Straight away, I was sent to detention.

Aston (Central Africa)

I came for business for only ten days to spend in UK. So I arrived in Heathrow Airport last year and they stopped my entry there. The following day, they brought me in Harmondsworth Centre, where I'm still detained until now.

I don't know why they brought me in that time. But the problem is that after being detained more than a month, like forty five days in detention, they came to me and say, "Okay, mister, we are sorry, we refuse you to enter in this country because we decided to cancel your visa."

So I told them that I don't know how you are working, but you are supposed to refuse my entry at the airport! So what am I doing is detention? Because I didn't come here to ask for asylum. I'm not I'm not an asylum seeker. So why I was detained?

Edgar (Central Africa)

I found myself in the United Kingdom. I was very happy to be where I could speak the language. I know the culture already. I knew I was somewhere safe. So I had to approach the authorities and told them this is what happened to me in Cameron, so I need your protection now. For the authorities to protect me? I found myself in detention.

Jay (Cameroon)

Now, the big issue is that while I was detained I had an accident in the detention centre and broke my ankle.

So I was waiting for surgery at the hospital but I don't know what happened with the doctor and the UKBA [UK Border Agency of the Home Office]. They stop my treatment and just say you have to go back and get the treatment done in your country.

So I told them, I didn't come here in crutches. I'm now disabled and I'm using crutches for over one year now. So I told them, I came here in a good health but now you are trying to send me back home with crutches. And I came here only to spend ten days. I have my own return ticket, I have my money, I have a reservation at the hotel. So why did you keep me here until I had an accident before you now tell me I can leave and you want to send me back home? So I told them I want justice because this is not very good.

It's not because I'm not a white man or because I'm black. They have to treat me like animal. So I've told them I want my treatment and go back home. So I don't know since then they just keep me here and nothing is done. And I'm still here now. It's been thirteen months today.

Edgar

Now, to be honest, compared to the severity of issues that I've experienced in my country, I didn't see that detention was a problem. I had seen people being killed in front of me, and knew I had survived. I've lost eleven members of my own family. So anything I was seeing at the airport was not a big thing.

In detention I can say I did see some incredible generosity, you know, like the police opening the small window-hatch and giving us something to eat. It was the first time I've seen bread with some leaves in between, and it made me think is this what people eat- like goats? They eat leaves?

It was quite funny. I had to take the leaves outside the bread and eat the rest.

But something which was shocking was that they asked me when I was born. And I stayed in detention for quite a long time simply because they were they were finding that I'm not credible, because I said I don't know when I was born. And seriously, I don't know when I was born. I know my mum went to find the firewood in the forest and had me. I'm not saying that she found me there! But that was the way I was born.

In a situation like in Congo, in the rainforest in the middle of nowhere, you know, it's too luxury to know when you're born. I know I was born in the rainy season. And I keep saying to them I was born in the rainy season. But they didn't want to believe me. And of course they go by ticking boxes.

Aston

I was detained in Harmandsworth. At first I took it as normal. That was an immigration detention. I said okay, maybe they want to check my background, to see if I'm from Cameroon, if truly I'm saying the truth about what's happened.

It took six months.

Jay

It's very simple just to send me back home. Why detain me? Now they have detained me over a year now. They have spent more than £90,000 pounds just keep me in the centre!

I broke my ankle in the detention centre. It was last November. In the corridor here the floor was wet so I slipped and broke my ankle. They call the ambulance and the ambulance came here to took me to the hospital. So I went to the hospital. They told me I was not in the system, or I don't know what they told each other there. So what they did in that time just giving me some pain medication and some crutches. And they say they will book another appointment for me and send me back to detention centre. After that, nothing is done, up to today.

I'm still on crutches. Every time I am in in my room on the bed. I can't walk.

When I went to the hospital, they didn't tell me nothing. They didn't tell me, "This is what's happening inside your ankle." They just talked to each other, between the officer, the jail company and the doctor. I don't know what they told each other.

So they just brought me back to the detention centre and tell me that in the next few weeks they will take me back to the hospital for an operation.

After some two months, three months, UKBA came in and say, "Okay, we want to remove you, and you can go back to your country and take that surgery in your country."

And I wrote a letter to them, I say, Okay, I came here in a good health, I was working, and I came here for business, I have my family back home, you detain me more than the time I supposed to spend in your country, so now I have an injury and you want to send me back like this? So, why? Am I an object or what? I am a human being!

They say no, because the doctor told them that if they make this operation it will take more than a year to recover. So this is the reason why they cannot do it here.

I say, ah-ha, so my health is not important for them!

So what is important for them now is just to send me back because they know that they make a mistake from beginning to detain me. So now they are trying many things to recover all those mistakes.

Edgar

On one fateful morning, after about two or three attempts to deport me unsuccessfully, one fateful morning I just saw him come in and he told me I'm leaving Harmandsworth for Portsmouth, to another detention centre. That was not an immigration detention centre. That was a prison. We all know Portsmouth prison is not an immigration detention centre. It's for criminals.

Jay

There was a guy here who died last year. They beat him. I was here.

There was one officer who beat him badly and what my concern is, they said this guy he wanted to go home. He was happy to go back to his country. So I don't know why they're treat him like this, until they kill him. For me, they killed him. Because someone who wanted to go home, why don't send him back home? You see? So why to keep him until he died, or you do something for him and he died? I don't know.

Edgar

So I was sent to Portsmouth and when I arrived I said to myself that it has happened, I just have to bear it. I've been in prison before, so I just have to face it. I tried.

Jay

I want to talk about indefinite detention. Somebody who comes through a bad situation in his own country comes here for humanitarian protection and you take him and you detain him! That is unbelievable.

That is appalling. We are not criminals.

And I see no reason why they should keep us with other criminals- people who have raped, people who have murdered, people who have done terrible crimes, it is no good at all.

John

My concern is I'm not a criminal. I have never been in this country before. I have never done any crime for this country. So why I will be detained over a year?

Even there is many criminals outside, they went to prison only six months, only three months, and they are outside already. What about me? I'm not a criminal! I didn't do anything! I've been detained over a year!

Edgar

I was very quick to react.

Since I went to Harmandsworth, I came to Refugee Radio just because I was at first searching for information, look who to contact, and that's how I came into contact with Stephen.

I was still in detention when I contacted Refugee Radio. So when I got to prison in Portsmouth, the very first day I asked for a computer. I needed to use the computer and internet. So what I discovered there was that, for you to use the computer, they have to give you a password before you log onto the system. [They give you] the password that you use. So whatever thing you do on that computer, they control it. You don't have any right to anything. So when they told me that, I went I just sent a short email to my solicitor, just to tell him where I was.

And that was it.

The guards saw the email and they came directly and shut off the computer.

The SIM they gave me was their own SIM. You don't have the right to your own SIM. Basically I had no communication, I had no privacy. I couldn't speak anything over the phone or over the Internet.

Jay

There's many, many, many things happen. Too many things is going on and the people doesn't know anything about it! Many things.

They keep people without no reason here. These people became crazy. You see people he is well today, next month or next two months, you will see he became crazy. He start to talk to himself.

In their life they never been having detention like it before. So they just came here and continue to spend more than a month in detention for no reason. And they are not a criminal. So why? I don't know.

Edgar

We are fighting to shut the detention system. Not just have a limit on them but shut them. We will demonstrate against detention. The power never concede anything if there is no demand. There are some detention centres that have closed but you've got to demand that they can shut them down. There is no use for them.

August

There is no healthcare here in the detention centre. No healthcare, I assure you.

Let me tell you something. You had a problem today, you say you want to see a doctor today, they will tell you to move to go and book for appointment. This appointment maybe will be one week before you see a doctor. So if you want to die today, after you die you will see a doctor? Or what?

You will see many, many detainees here, you will see, they are crying, they have so much problem, they have a headache, they have this problem, but nothing done. They will tell them just go and take paracetamol in the office. That's it.

Edgar

You don't know nothing. If you will die here, you don't know. You don't know nothing, you don't know. And they just keep making money on your behalf. The only thing is business. Only thing they are making a profit.

Edgar

Luckily enough, the following morning came and we did some few paperwork. And I was released for temporary admission. And I found myself into the community. I started to volunteer. I said I want to help my community, I need to give back to the community. So I contacted the Red Cross and there's another charity in London that I tried to visit those in prison, which I still do to today. So I've been doing the activism since I left detention.

Jay

The only thing I can say is that, for me, this UKBA is criminals.

They're criminals because how people who are not a criminal who didn't do nothing, who didn't came from prison, can be detained over a year? Is not only me, I know many people who have been here over a year, two years, three years in this centre. And they didn't come from prison, only maybe they are illegally in this country, or they say they want to sell them back home. So if you cannot send them back home, why don't you leave them pending their removal direction?

So what have they done to be detained over two years, three years in the centre? For what?

So I think they have to review all the system. For people to be detained over a year is no good. Because I don't know, I don't know, I don't know... is like to torture them, torture them mentally. Because every day you think you will get released tomorrow. And if you don't get release you can be crazy.

When you went to the prison, you'll know that you went to the prison today, and you will be out on next six months or next year or the next three months, I don't know, but here, you enter this place and you don't know when or where or how you will get out for this place.

Edgar

Detention- Notes

The United Nations Convention relating to the Status of Refugees (1951) recognises that "the seeking of asylum can require refugees to breach immigration rules. Prohibited penalties might include being charged with immigration or criminal offences relating to the seeking of asylum, or being arbitrarily detained purely on the basis of seeking asylum."

It is not easy to square this with the UK's immigration rules which carry a penalty of four year's imprisonment for 'illegally entering' the UK, especially when there is no way to legally enter the UK to claim asylum.

It is also difficult to square the 1951 Convention with the routine detention of asylum seekers for administrative purposes.

Many of our respondents were put into detention centres when they claimed asylum, and removal centres when they were refused asylum. The difference between a centre and a prison is fairly negligible, according to the people who have been imprisoned in them. In some senses, they are worse. A few years ago, the government's Chief Inspector of Prisons said that Yarl's Wood removal centre was a "place of national concern." When the United Nations sent their Special Rapporteur on Violence Against Women to investigate complaints about sexual abuse by male staff against female detainees, she was not even allowed into the building. A BBC Panorama documentary in 2017 revealed a widespread culture of disdain and disrespect among the staff towards the detainees, culminating in routine bullying and violence.

We reported on the situation in a previous book, Refugee Radio Times (2014):

"In 2012, a 31-year-old Ghanaian man called Prince Ofosu died after being 'restrained' by GEO Group staff at Harmondsworth Immigration Removal Centre (IRC). A statement from other Ghanaian detainees at the centre alleged that Ofosu sustained massive blows from one officer who later asked to change his "blood-stained clothes so that no one would notice what happened", and that the officer concerned was put on leave "in order to pervert the course of justice". After

the beating, which happened in a solitary confinement room, they say that they were told by another officer who was present that Ofusu was stripped naked, the heating was turned off, and he was "left in the cold without even a duvet till his death 24 hours after being detained at the block". The statement also makes allegations about the mistreatment of other Ghanaians, and the lack of proper medical care at the centre where there is no permanent doctor (as is frequently the case at detention centres). There was no proper police investigation of his death, which was referred to the Prisons and Probation Ombudsman.

"The asylum seekers we have spoken to tell us that they are also invariably mistreated during removal. They are racially abused and beaten by the guards, sometimes in the van on the way to the aeroplane, sometimes on the plane itself and sometimes in the van on the way back to the centre from the plane - occasionally flights are postponed if the pilot objects too much to all the violence. A Cameroonian man who was trafficked into slavery as a child told us he was punched in the groin and needed medical attention. Another Cameroonian man, Marius Betondi, was beaten so hard he received serious injuries to his eyes and face. Seven months later, an Angolan man, Jimmy Mubenga, was killed by three G4S guards at the same airport."

One of the biggest differences between detention and prison is the policy of "indefinite detention", where asylum seekers are locked up for years at a time with no end date in sight. As our respondent Edgar explains: "When you went to the prison, you'll know that you went to the prison today, and you will be out in the next six months or next year or the next three months, I don't know. But here, you enter this place and you don't know when or where or how you will get out for this place."

Indefinite detention flies in the face of basic principles of liberty and justice. It is arguably in violation of the Human Rights Act and the European Convention on Human Rights.

There were between 20,000 and 30,000 people a year going into detention before Covid hit. The numbers fell sharply as a result of the lockdown but are now returning to previous levels. These figures used to include 1,000 children as well, but in 2010 the Coalition government announced that they would end child detention. They opened a house called Cedars Pre-Departure Accommodation with the children's charity, Barnardo's, and promised to do things differently from now on. However, Cedars was closed a few years later and the children were just moved to Tinsley House Immigration Removal Centre, outside Gatwick Airport.

Like the decision to prevent asylum seekers from working, detention costs a lot of money to run.

Similarly, the policy is based on an untested assumption that the alternative would be worse, an assumption that is never brought into question because detention makes asylum seekers suffer and is therefore part of a "tough" government stance. The work of running the centres has been outsourced to multinational corporations such as Serco and G4S, who run them for a profit.

The breakdown of people entering detention reveals that your likelihood of being detained depends on your country of origin. People from India, Nigeria and China are far more likely to be detained. They are held at disproportionate levels to the numbers of people coming from those countries. Indians are the second most common detainees but only just make the top ten for asylum applicants in the last decade. China is not even in the top ten. On the other hand, people from Iran, Afghanistan and Iraq are conversely significant in asylum applications but relatively less likely to be detained. Some of this can be explained by visa overstayers, and some by the difficulty of arranging return flights to places like Afghanistan, but a lot of the discrepancies are mysterious.

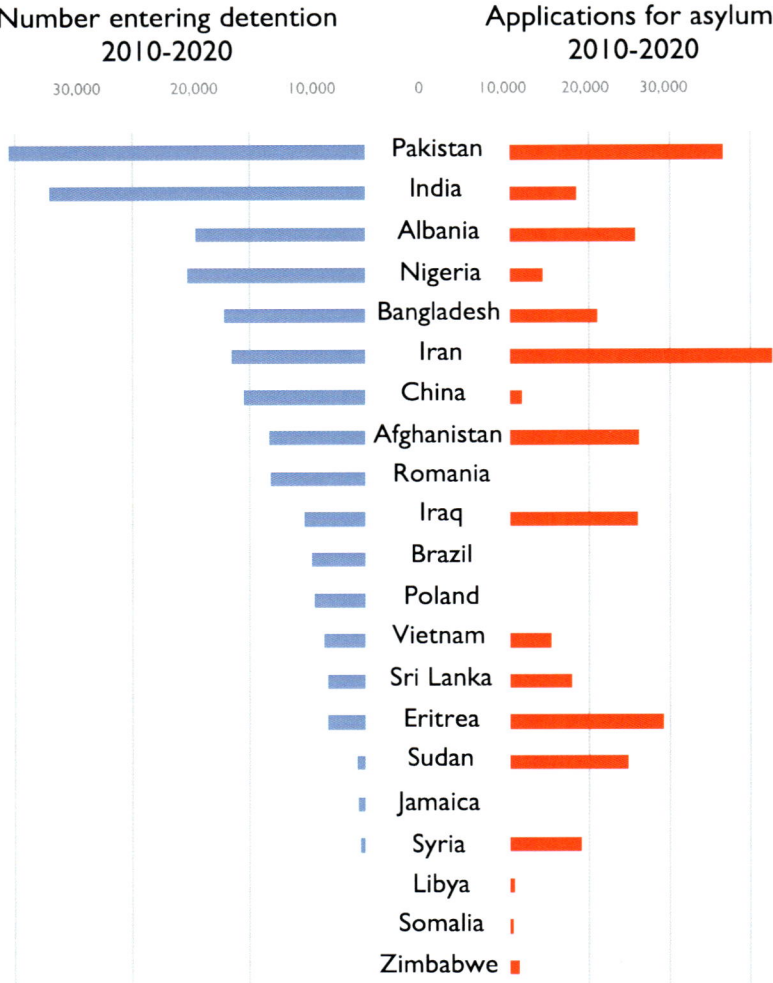

Number entering detention 2010-2020				Applications for asylum 2010-2020		
30,000	20,000	10,000	0	10,000	20,000	30,000

Country of origin comparrison for people enterring detention vs asylum applications 2010-2020

(Note: a zero indicates no data available, as these numbers were so low that they were below the threshold of monitoring. Figures from The Migration Observatory at the University of Oxford 2021 compared with our analysis of Home Office asylum and resettlement datasheets).

Claiming asylum

The UK border agents take a long time to decide on your case. And you don't know what to do. And you don't have anything else to do. You just sit at home and rot like a cabbage.

Rose

The first day I arrived to the UK I was hoping- "I came to the UK, so now I will find support, all my everything, and I will see my family, because my family I left in my country."

At the start they told me to stay in London for three months in a camp and then they transferred me to Brighton. And as like day after day, month after month, a year comes, and I was like, what's going on? Okay?

I came with bad mental health, with bad health.

Saleh

If they don't want us then, they should tell us to go at the start of the process.

When we seek asylum, I think it is very due and good enough if we've been refused immediately and sent back rather than to stay here for one year, two years, three and four years. And at the end of the day, we're still not hearing news about our cases.

Rose

I was thirteen. They put me with these people [foster carers]. I was really, really tired so I had to sleep like two days. When I get to them house they giving me some food. They had a chat with me and get to know me. And after that I can have a shower and they giving me some clothes. And after that I went to sleep. So I sleep till next day one o'clock, two o'clock, because I was really tired, I couldn't sleep most of the time. This is the first time I sleep and I feel safe. Nobody can come wake me up, pull me somewhere, take me somewhere. And after that I wake up, they make some lunch for me, they are making some pizza. This is the first time I eat pizza and I don't know what is it!

Mostafa

You keep us waiting for that long time and we come more, like, bad mental health. I was just waiting, I was really worried about my family, they were between the dangerous things in my country and I couldn't sleep, all the time I was thinking for my family and also thinking when I will get the interview at the Home Office. It's really like, take long time, and I don't know why.

Saleh

All the asylum seekers they are suffering from the Home Office.

June

It was in Slough. For the first five months, six months they [foster carers] was really, really nice. And after that they get changed. They're not nicer to me anymore. If I go outside they told me I have to come back early, not to say, maximum six o'clock, seven o'clock I have to be home. At first she was asking me what's the food I like so she can make it and after that she stopped asking and she make the food … and I don't like it. It's not that I don't like it, but they put stuff on it, like ingredients, I don't like it.

I start to hate to go there because there are lots of children because they keep bullying and making noise and I don't like it. And I don't know how to speak English and I don't know what they're speaking about.

Mostafa

I don't know why. It's like they keep us waiting for a long time and they can't decide. We put more bad situation. It's really like they don't feel how we were in our bad situation. I really I haven't find such bad days in all my life. Just, I was waiting for my interview, I was waiting for my family, I was waiting for my operation, it's like a lot of things like comes and make it hard for us.

Saleh

They was worried that I go out again and get lost, so each time I go outside they get somebody to go with me. If I want to go shopping, whatever, they send somebody with me. My social worker come and ask what happened. I told her everything. She said, "Okay, you're going to leave here now, don't worry. We're going to get your stuffs." That's it. So they put me in a shared house. I lived for this house one year and a half.

They were like my age, seventeen, eighteen, this age. We just shared everything, like, we shared the kitchen. Everyone has his own room. The toilet or bathroom we share it together. There was two people from here, UK, and the other two from Ethiopia, and the other guy is from another land than me. The first two looked British, I asking them and they say, we're from here. It was one guy and one girl. We didn't get on with each other. If they need anything from you they just ask you, that's it. First time I introduced myself to them and asking their names, and that's it. No more talking.

But he was friendly with me, the Afghani guy. He was a friend of me. We was going out sometimes. And the Ethiopian guys was in the same college as me. Same class as well. I lived there about one year, one year and a half. I turned seventeen in this house and after that when I was eighteen my case been closed because I don't have enough evidence.

Mostafa

I think the biggest problem is Home Office taking so long to deal with cases. If they dealt with cases in the short timespan. I think will be less of burdens to the country.

Rose

Social services said, "We can't help you anymore, you're out of under social services." After that they moved me to London. I feel so sad and mad. I got lots of depressions. Before I leave the shared house, they said they want to sending me back to my country. I told them I don't want to go back and I haven't got anybody there to go back to.

Mostafa

And well, we are all stressed up. We're just like…
you don't know what you're doing, really whether
you are going or coming. So that's the main problem
which I think some of the asylum seekers face.

Rose

So I have this very close friend of mine who lives
in the States. He's always been a brother to me. He
said, "No. You can't go back home. Do you know
what is asylum?"

To be very honest with you, honestly speaking,
I've been in this country to study. I've heard of asylum
but I really never ever took time to read what it is or
how it works or anything. I was like, "No."

He was like, "You need to seek an asylum."

And I was like, "How do I do that? My visa runs
out in, what, ten days! Where do I start?"

And he was like, "You need to call, you need to
Google it, you need to make calls. I don't know how it
works in England, but you need to Google it."

He literally took two days to convince me,
together with my mum. And I finally called the Home
Office and they told me to come in to Croydon.

So I had to go down to Croydon, where I told
them I wanted to seek asylum. They asked why, and
I said because of my sexuality. They said, okay, we're
gonna start the screening process. All through that day
I still didn't even know what I was doing, to be honest.

I was panicking, I was scared, I was shaking, I was... I was lost. Because the person I loved had just left me and she wouldn't even call me. She won't text me. She just left me like that. So I was left all by myself. No family, nothing, nothing.

I always thought deep down that I was going to reconcile with her. That she was going to call me back and tell me she's sorry and let's continue. But she's never done that. She's never done that. On Saturday it was my birthday and that was the first time I heard from her, when she texted me "happy birthday," that's all.

Right now I'm in a bit of a difficult time in my life where I want to be able to live a normal life and be in love with who I want to be with, and work, and do things. But now I'm stuck. I'm waiting on the Home Office to process with my asylum claim. But I'm happy I'm in a society which is open to being lesbian. I don't feel unsafe. I'm happy and I'm free.

What I would say to other people in my situation is, to be honest- don't be scared, be strong. When you know what you want, always follow what make yourself happy. So there's a lot of people in the same situation, but what they do is they just say, oh, you know what, I'm gonna keep myself unhappy, pretend till we get through everything. But when you get to that point where you can't pretend to be happy to please people: do what is right.

You have every right to be lesbian or gay. It's not a bad thing. It's normal thing. So don't be scared. Be proud of who you are. Go for it.

Patience

My asylum application is still pending at the Home Office. They've not yet made a decision. So I'm still waiting to hear from them. But it's clear that I've been here for twelve years, and that has compounded my misery. I believe that the most important thing is what I believe and what I stand for. But I said I feel that I have been persecuted again because of what I'm going through here that I have no status. I have no life. You know, I feel that I'm losing.

And to be honest with you, my active life is running out. I have not been able to do anything with my life for the past four years because I have no status. You understand? And that is so hurting for me.

I was brought up in the culture of working to provide for yourself. That's the way I was brought up. All these things called "benefits" here and I don't know anything about it and I don't want it. I want to work and provide for my family and provide for this nation. That is my fervent wish, to be able to highlight the British traditional policy of helping those in need. I want to support this economy.

You've come here to my home and you've seen the state I live in with my family. It is unbelievable that somebody has got a son and a wife is living in one room in a shared accommodation like this. This is… how do I begin to understand… how do I begin to live with the conditions I face here? And with what I faced in Cameroon? It's really hard on me.

Sometimes, I'll be honest, sometimes I felt suicidal. Sometimes I have done that before. I've done that. But Thank God my wife was here. When I've had enough of life and say let me, let me go away, but my wife was there to rescue me.

It's not been easy for me at all. It's not been easy. You see... you walk down the street, you have friends and you can see them moving on with their lives, making contribution to the economy, changing their life, making something better with their life and I look at myself: I'm just in limbo. I'm lost. I'm so hollow. I'm so empty.

John

If you don't have status, every time you live in fear. You don't know. You're not entitled for anything. And anytime they can come and grab you and take you back home, which is like very dangerous.

So you be living in fear. And you can't sleep. You'll be having a lot of nightmares because you don't know what is next.

But at the moment I've got my status. I feel more better. Now I'm entitled to get some help, I can go to the GP and get some medicine.

Now I'm waiting to go to college. Before you go trying but it's: "You are not entitled, sorry." Everywhere you go they say: "Oh, sorry." You understand that but you are not entitled. So you feel like you're not part of the community or you're not part of the people.

Paul (East Africa)

I don't have money. The government didn't give me money. Almost the first one and a half year, they are just arguing with me that I'm having money in my account in my country, which it is not correct!

June

As an asylum seeker I'm really blessed I'm in a system, but the sad part is that I don't have work permit. But Migrant Help are helping me with the weekly food money, now forty pound weekly from this week. And also they can give me accommodation but I didn't go their accommodation, because they will send me very far, far, place, rural area. I just want to be stay with the friends. I like to show Home Office I'm in an artist's community, they are helping me, supporting me, and I'm doing my practice so I don't want to be go accommodation where it is very isolated place.

Kajoli

I was advised by the friends to apply for asylum on the basis of my sexuality. Before I got here, I didn't know about it, that you can claim asylum on the basis of your sexuality. I applied and it got rejected. They took me to the court and it got thrown out as well.

The Home Office told me you have to keep signing on as we are preparing for you to go back. I said to myself, okay. I didn't go to sign on. I absconded. I ran away. Over the next nine years, I lived in hiding because I didn't want them to take me back in Uganda.

August

I make a fresh claim which the lawyer he is helping me, because the lawyer from the government she is not a nice lady, which is she spoiled all my case. And so I found the new lawyer, he is a private lawyer but he is a nice and a good man. He make a fresh claim for me, and he took all the documents he wanted. I almost stay for two years to answer me about my fresh claim. Nothing.

Suddenly, I heard that they refuse my fresh claim. I went to the court and the Home Office officer he is so nasty, nasty, nasty, as much as you can.

June

I just want to send a message. This message goes to the Home Office, the immigration UK Border Control. They need to treat the refugee and asylum seeker as the human being.

They don't need to treat us like criminal, because when they catch you and they got you somewhere, they treat us all as a criminal. Then you feel yourself like, oh maybe I'm not a human being, the way they do things and shout at you. You don't have even right to… they just treat us bad.

So I think if they can change for that, because we come out of our country and it is not a choice. Some of us, we left because of the problem which is something I cannot go into too much details about.

Paul

You see even they threaten me that with one bullet we can kill you. I was so scared that for almost one month I didn't move from home, I didn't open window, I didn't open the door, I just eat what I have at home and I'm scared to go out alone. So I decide to go abroad. My other son he didn't got his paper yet, but the one who's here [in the UK] already has his paper. So I said I'll go and visit him. If I like to stay, I'll stay. If no, I'll come back.

When I came, they told me there is no chance that you think. No way that if you decide, or you don't decide: you're not going back. So just from the time I arrived, I applied second day by telephone to the Home Office that I want to apply for asylum seeker. They sent for me a letter for the appointment and when I went there I was so scared.

I suffered from it. So I'm having my healths, it's not okay: depression, anxiety, PTSD. And I'm not eating, I'm not sleeping, I'm so worried, I'm scared to go out. In my country, you cannot sleep in a home with a glass window like the ones they have here. No. There is iron bars. You have to protect yourself, otherwise you will find that people come inside and they try to kill you. So, for a long time, I couldn't sleep. I'm scared someone will come from the window, which is normal here to leave like that.

But I didn't get my status. I'm scared that they will return me back home and I thought that they will give me my status quickly. I find that they refuse me. They refuse my case.

June

So you end up you're here, and you say, okay, let me stay here to save my life. But when you come here like I'm come here, to just rescue myself, and you start treating me bad, then it makes us to be like knock our confidence, go depression and mental. Because if a person come to help you and the person that treats you bad, that is really bad, so they need to be [helpful] if someone is asylum seeker, we need some care. We are human.

Paul

The lady, the advisor there of police [Home Office interviewing officer], what is her name? I don't remember. The one, she's asking me the questions in the second interview, she was so nasty with me, and I suffer so much. Almost staying there for six hours. She just give me five minutes because I told her, I'm diabetic, and I need to go to the toilet. "Five minutes only. Not more than that."

And she is sitting eating chocolates and biscuits and answered the telephone. And she refused to make the tape for me. She just write what she want to write. And because I don't have a lawyer, nobody told me that I have to check what she wrote within five days. So after that, I discovered that she wrote a nasty thing. She just lied. Even the interpreter she told her, "You are not going to make a tape?"

She said, "No. I am not going to make a tape. It's up to me."

And there is a people outside they told me one made his interview and I found he has the CD. Yeah, I told him what is this? He said that the CD or the Flash Drive, they have to give it to you. So she put it in mind that I can ask. I told her you're not going to record it? She said, "No. it's up to me." She's a Pakistani. I think she is a racist. And what she wrote it, it show what she's feeling against me, [religious discrimination], yes.

June

I remember one time I went to sign on. That one I cannot forget. I missed the date to sign on in the Home Office in Croydon. I need to sign every week, but I missed it one week because that time they don't give me money for travel ticket.

When the man told me, he was proper, proper English- triple typical English. And I go there and queue, queue, queue. Yes, go: Hello, mister. How are you?

"I'm fine. Thank you. What's your name?"

I talk my name and date of birth.

Check on the system. He say, "Oh." He just look at me with the intimidation face. "You Paul?"

Yes.

"From [East Africa]?"

Yes.

"Why did you miss sign? You need to come and sign!"

Yes. I didn't get a travel ticket for train. That's why I didn't turn up.

"What do you mean you didn't get it?"

I said yeah, they used to give me ticket, but that time they didn't send me tickets. So that's why, mister. So, when I get the ticket, that's why I come today.

"Do you know you can be detained?"

I was scared. Because I know what I pass through. I was scared even when I talk about that. I feel so…

I say I know. But it wasn't my choice. I want to come but I live really far away.

And he look at me up and down and say, "Why you come in this country? And you know you can't afford the ticket to come here to sign? Why you come here?"

I said, no, sir, it wasn't my choice to come in this country. I was having some problem.

And after he say, "Why don't you sell that hat?"

I was wearing a Nike baseball cap.

"Why don't you sell that hat so then you can get money to get the travel ticket?"

And that hat, I got it for free from a charity because I used to go to charity to give me some clothes.

And he told me, "Sit on that side there."

Me I was thinking, now I'm going to see maybe two men come and say, "Okay you're going to be detained."

But I waited, and, after talking to some other people, he come back here. He say, "Next time if you know you don't have money, you need to sell something you have, like your hat, so you can get money to sign on. Or you should stay in your country."

Paul

173

Because the interpreter she was so nice. Can you think about six hours without drinking and I'm diabetic? What's happened to me? Suddenly, I have hypoglycemia. The interpreter, she gave me her juice. And that one [Home Office interviewing officer], she refused to stop the meeting. So after the six hours, when I'm going, my son is waiting me outside. And that day it was raining and cold and it is -2°C in Croydon and just I went out, I was crying. It's not easy to sit six hours with that person treating me very bad like that.

She doesn't believe one word from what I'm saying! She's telling me, "By the way, I don't believe you."

I told her why?

She said, "I have my friend. She go to your country. And she is all the time she is happy."

I told her is she like me [Coptic Christian]?

She told me, "Of course no."

I told her, "Of course she will be happy. She will be very happy there!"

You see, they want me to come to the Home Office every two weeks to sign. So the police officer, when he's filling the form, he told me you have to come every two weeks. The police officer.

A lady sit near him. She told him, "Did you read her age? Date of birth?"

So he said, "Ah okay."

She told him, "Let her come up every one months." So I have to go every months.

June

I was feeling so…

When I was coming back in the train that was the day I feel like… this life is really bad. Because you come here when you think you are in trouble there. So you come here to save your life and you find some people like this.

Paul

I remember one day, I was waiting for two hours. First of all, they treat us very, very, very bad. As if we are as slaves. Shouting at us. For example, if I enter inside, I just go a little bit from the queue? They shout "You go inside! Go inside, you nasty lady!" So of course, I cannot complain or shout or anything.

So after two hours waiting to give me the ticket, when I asked, I said, What about the ticket?

He said, "A moment."

Suddenly there is two police guy, one come in front, one at the back. "There is interview for you."

What interview? I didn't know that you are going to make an interview?

"No. We are doing an interview for you."

So, they took me in the same floor, in another department, and start checking me by hand. And they took my bag. They took my watch, my earrings, and my ring! I don't know what is the reason for that. So they took me in a room and close it inside by the key. I felt that I am a criminal, that I have done something wrong when I'm sitting at the Home Office. Suddenly, he has a six pages questions. And I answer him. So you see I'm diabetic. I asked him, I need to go to the loo. So he went with me and checked the toilet.

And he let me enter inside and wait me inside, not outside! And again, when I come back, they check me again! So he insists that they will drop me from Home Office, Croydon, back to my country. So I start crying.

I told him, I cannot go to my country. They will kill me. Several times I have to tell him that they will kill me.

He insist, "No problem. We'll get the ticket for you."

I told him, You don't understand what I'm saying. They will kill me! And I start crying.

He told me, "Okay, this is my card. If you decide to go and you don't have money, just call me."

Of course I'm in a bad mood because of the bad situation. And at that time I was living outside of Brighton [with a family as part of a refugee hosting scheme]. I lost the first train going to the place where I was living with the family. And when I reached there, I could not find the place because I was so upset. I don't know where is the home. I have to call the lady [from the family] and tell her come and pick me from the station. Of course I didn't sleep at night. I was crying, shouting. And her room was near my room. She has to woke up and cool me down.

And anytime I see a police car I was scared and shaking. And she told me, "Don't worry, I'm with you." I told her, they might come and pick me and drop me to my country, which I am scared to go there.

June

So this is my message for the Home Office: they need to treat us like we are human.

And they need to know we are here not because of our choice. Some of us like me, because I wouldn't like to separate with my family, my lovely daughter there, and all people around me, to be coming here to be like...

So we need at least some care. That's the message I can give to the UK Border Control Immigration, because I think there is a lot of people who have passed through a lot and they don't have that chance, but me to get this my voice- if you reach to them? That would be nice.

We are human. Thank you very much.

Paul

By the way, the dog they're treating very well. They treat you as a slave. You are coming to take their country. You are going to stole something from their country. I don't know why they are like that. Some companies or government they have, but I think this is their attitude there.

You cannot change them. If you're lucky, you get your status quickly and get rid of them.

June

I've never felt safe until I got to the UK. In the past, in Burma, in refugee camp, and even in Bangkok,

I always lived in constant fear. First because I was afraid of attack. Even in refugee camp, we were attacked by the Burmese troops. And in even in Bangkok, because I didn't have any proper document, no identity cards, no passport. I lived as a ghost citizen. So my life was always with fear.

When I got to the UK I felt safer, and, at night, I could sleep properly and without worrying that I would be attacked. And I could sleep until the morning.

Then I was asylum seeker and I had to wait for two years. Because I couldn't go back to Burma, I had no choice, but to apply for asylum because of my political activities. And after I got asylum here, I was recognised as a refugee. And this is the day where I felt safe in my life, I felt like I became a proper human.

Mima

I think somebody is maybe talking about some problems like when the Home Office lost your file. It's not good. Feels not comfortable.

Rose

I think the system is already good, because I think it is important to understand why people come to the UK, and then claimed asylum, and why it is important to provide sanctuary and refuge for people like myself and others who have been forced to flee from their homeland.

But I think it's also important to implement the system very carefully, so that you don't make much mistake. For example, with my case, I had to wait for two years. And every week I had to go to the police station; I had to sign my name, and I wasn't allowed to work, and I wasn't allowed to have a bank account, and life was so difficult for me as asylum seeker.

My life from a big jungle, in refugee camp, and then to a big city in the UK, was full with challenge and surprise. And sometimes I would cry at night, thinking how difficult life was. But then I thought: I had to survive, I had to face this challenge to be able to survive for another day.

Mima

When we seek asylum here in this country, it's like it's a crime. We've been treated like some people who have got convictions, some criminals as well. The reason is this- you are not allowed to work. Some of us don't get support. We're not allowed to work. And even sometimes when we are sick, we're being forced to come into the Home Office to report, which I don't think it is appropriate. Yeah. Because I think UK as a country should be a fair country for all. And if it's a diverse country, and then people have been treated differently. I don't think it's really very good. We are an asylum seeker. It's not a crime. We are not criminals. I think we deserve some respect, as well. And we deserve support.

Rose

But despite these challenges, refugees have never stopped trying to make the UK their new home. They have never been docile nor unproductive. There is no doubt refugees make a huge contribution to the UK life and economy. So it's sad that the UK asylum system is not using the potential and capacities of the refugees for a positive change.

Yusef

I wish and I hope that the Home Office try to be good with the people. This is what I wish it. Because you see, nobody will leave his country to come and live here that you treat us like that. We are visitors at your country, you have to treat us better.

By the way they are not British, what they are doing. They put the workers who are Pakistani, Afghani, Irani, how they treat you in Home Office. But if you find the British they are so nice.

You see, when I was sick, and I brought the letter from my GP asking them that I can go every three months. The lady there, she's Iranian, "No, I'm not going to give you the three months. I'll give you two months only."

When I enter and I find me that I'm not a young girl. And there is, I remember, once, he let me stay for one hour to take the lift and go and make to sign. And when I looked at him, he pretend to be busy like that. He let some people come after me, they go, and let me stay. Even I'm not a young girl, and I'm with my wheelchair. And he refused for me to take the lift. And there is another one, he come before, he's shouting at us, he's Afghani or something like that. "Why you are sitting till now? It is one hour you're sitting."

I told him, "Ask him. He doesn't want me to take the lift now."

So someone told me that the Home Office pretend to do that. Why? To let you hate, hate, to stay in the country. So you will say, I'll go by myself back to my country. Even I'm suffering there, but it's better than that they treat me here like that.

June

The Nationality and Borders Bill allows the government to set up new detention facilities outside of the UK. The people will be taken and locked up while their asylum claims are processed. This offshore policy, like the Australian model, will result in child and sexual abuse and a considerable cost to the public purse.

Part of the problem is that gender isn't listed as a reason for persecution in the Refugee Convention. And I would like to ask why it isn't? Why, while there are countries like Iran, where half the population, women, are living under sexual apartheid?

One aspect of this law is that it expects asylum seekers to tell everything on their arrival. And if they add something later, the authorities won't accept. But women often don't talk about issues such as rape that they've suffered, not on their first interview, or even their last interview. I know Iranian women here who have their refugee status, who were raped in prison, but never talked about it in their asylum interviews.

They were lucky that they came at the time that claiming refugee status wasn't as difficult as now.

Shame, and the fear of what their family or their community might think, prevented them from revealing that aspect of what had happened to them in prison. So the Bill punishes traumatised women who aren't able to share their whole story when they first come to the UK.

Many women need mental health support, proper legal advice, and to feel safe before they can open up about the violence and abuse they have fled.

Yasmin

Sometimes, some of them have been rejected, and then they are at the periphery of the society because they are hiding from the authorities. They still some of them have families. So they cannot work, they cannot do anything, yet they still need assistance. So I also have a network of faith-based organisations and these are some of the people that we also assist, giving them sometimes a place to stay, and sometimes food. We have supermarkets, big supermarkets here, so we have the voucher so they can go and buy anything they want. And then if money is left, they can still save the card and then use it again and again.

So these are some of the things that we are doing at the basic level. But again, like you will notice, refugees and migrants generally since the migrant crisis that happened in 2003 are facing a lot of difficulties- discrimination, prejudice, racism, xenophobia, it is a difficult moment. And of course, I've gone through this, and sometimes I sit and I listen to stories, and I try to guide people. When you listen, it just breaks your heart what is going on.

Idris

I swear- my wife every day, just cry; every night.

Edgar

I am a refugee and I've got refugee status. I come from Southern Cameroon. I've lived here for more than sixteen years now, close to seventeen years. I was in limbo for more than fifteen years, and it has taken a toll on my life.

I've got two kids born in this country. It is a challenge.

What is failing us asylum seekers is the system. The system is very old. The system is very dehumanising, I will say it. Do you understand?

And one thing I don't understand- we need to start asking ourselves, why does the British government does not allow asylum seekers to be given the entitlement to work?

One: to fend for themselves.

Two: to contribute to the economy and to make this country a better place.

In the United States, when you seek asylum, you don't depend on the government. They immediately give you the right to work, to take care of yourself and to support the system. In the meantime, they process applications as much as it is in Germany and other European countries. But here is it is different. Why not allow us to work while you process our application and we can contribute to the economy? We have to support ourselves.

When you begin to allow people to live on this culture of depending on the state, if you give them status then they don't want to work anymore!

Britain is on the verge of starving. There are cuts day in, day out. There are a lot of people who need help in this country, people who are disabled in this country and the government cannot care for them, yet the government is wasting money on asylum seekers when they should be giving them that right. Just say, "Okay, I'm going to process your application but I'll give you the right to work to support us and to support the system." They don't do it. There is something we need to talk about it. Really. The system is no good at all.

John

Claiming asylum- Notes

Claiming asylum is the start of a Kafkaesque ordeal that will consume years of your life.

It is not possible to claim asylum from outside of the country and you are expected to make a claim as soon as you arrive, for example at passport control. If you delay in making your claim then the Home Office may argue that your case is not genuine. This is one of the first things that you learn about the process- it is adversarial. The Home Office presumes that everyone is guilty before being proved innocent, and will constantly be looking for reasons to dismiss your claim.

You have to make an appointment by phone if you have not been able to claim on arrival. Except that our respondents tell us that you can never get through on the phone line and nobody ever answers. You're supposed to be able to claim in person if you are homeless by going to the Intake Unit in Croydon, but in practice our clients have just been turned away.

If you do get through the front door, you will have a screening interview. The immigration officer will ask you why you are claiming asylum. This interview takes place in a public area and you may feel unable to disclose private information about your case such as torture or sexual assault. The Home Office will use this against you if you try to talk about these things later. The interview is not recorded, and the interviewing officer may write down something different to what you have told them. You won't know that this is happening and the Home Office will use this against you. Then they process your biometric data for their records– fingerprints, photographs, iris scans etc.

This is followed by your substantive interview, which takes several hours and goes into more detail. You might have to wait a year or two for this interview to happen. Afterward, you might have to wait six months or more for a decision.

During this time, you are not allowed to work. Anyone caught employing an asylum seeker can face up to five years in prison and have to pay an unlimited fine. Any asylum seeker caught working can also be sent to prison.

You are not allowed to claim benefits either. You are expected to have arrived in the UK with enough resources to support yourself for however many years it takes to process your claim.

If you are homeless and without money, you can apply for asylum support from the Home Office.

You have to be able to convince them that you are destitute, however, and they may not believe you, as was the case with our respondent, June: "Almost the first one and a half year, they are just arguing with me that I'm having money in my account in my country, which it is not correct!"

The support comes in the form of a special card, which tracks your location and sends the details to the Home Office every time you use it. They can use this information against you. You get £40.85 per week. For reference this is just 55% of the £77.28 per week that you get on Universal Credit, which is, it is worth noting, the minimum amount of money that the government determines you need to live on so that you do not starve.

The accommodation is offered on a no-choice dispersal basis. This means that the Home Office will send you to a place somewhere in the UK and you have to take it or leave it. Dispersal accommodation is mostly in the poorest areas of the Midlands and the North. The policy was purportedly introduced to reduce demand on services in London, but it has the effect of frustrating refugee communities from establishing themselves in the way that settled migrants rely upon. The properties generally take the form of single rooms in overcrowded shared houses with unsanitary conditions and are managed by private companies for profit (G4S, Clearsprings and Serco). It is low-quality housing that you would not be able to rent to people on the private market. In the north-east, you can tell where the asylum seekers live because the doors of their houses are all bright red.

If you're unlucky, you might get housed somewhere like Napier Barracks, a semi-derelict site that had been abandoned by the military for over fifteen years before it was used as temporary accommodation for hundreds of asylum seekers.

There are no facilities for people with special needs and no care for people with mental-health issues. If someone is actively suicidal then you can telephone Migrant Help, a charity that has been outsourced by the Home Office to administer asylum support. In the whole time that Brighton has been a dispersal area, Migrant Help have never once visited anyone in person. Every safeguarding concern we have raised has just resulted in them telephoning the person once to see if they are still alive and then taking no further action. No face-to-face contact, no referral to mental-health services, no nothing. Migrant Help's contract is worth £20,000,000 per year to the taxpayer.

While you are seeking asylum, you may be asked to report to the Home Office. Our respondents told us about being asked to go to "sign" at Lunar House in Croydon every month. Every time they attended there was the possibility that they might not come out again. Being asked to go into a separate room after signing could mean a simple interrogation or it could mean you were being detained.

Some people are asked to go more frequently.

I once interviewed the asylum-seeking playwright, Lydia Besong on the bus as she was travelling to report to the Home Office. It was a journey of several hours involving multiple buses. Lydia had angered the Home Office by staging a play that was critical of the system (How I Became an Asylum Seeker, 2009) and she was being asked to report every single day. Before that, she had been detained and threatened with removal.

Detention can happen at any point of your asylum journey. It is often done for "administrative convenience" and the Home Office does not need to give you a reason. You do not have the right to freedom.

Part Three: Life in the UK

"Learn to be a permanent prisoner of hope."
Idris

Life in the UK- Notes

As our respondent, Oba, tells us, "I never know when being refugee stops." The journey does not simply come to an end after someone has claimed asylum and settled in the UK.

The final part of this book looks at what happens next. It is named after the Life in the UK Test, a computer-based quiz that you have to pass before you can naturalise as a British Citizen. It was introduced alongside an English-language test twenty years ago, supposedly as a way to ensure that people who want to become British share the same level of knowledge about the country as those who were born here. In practice, it is an arcane set of crypto-nationalist hurdles determined seemingly at random by privately educated civil servants that resembles a Pub Quiz set in Hell.

Many of the questions in the test require applicants to know things that would puzzle the majority of British natives:

- *Which British monarch empowered the central administration of Parliament during their reign, thereby severely restricting the power of the nobility, who had previously ruled the nation?*
- *In addition to Protestantism, Henry VII tried to impose which law in Ireland, resulting in the Irish Chieftains rebellion?*
- *Who did Henry VII defeat in order to become the first Tudor King?*
- *During the middle of the 14th Century there was a shortage of field workers resulting in rises in the cost of labour. What was the reason for this shortage of labour?*
- *In which year was the independence of American Colonies recognised?*
- *For over a century, religious intolerance prevailed all over Europe, one cause of which was the division of Ireland. How would you classify the reason?*
- *What was "The Butler Act" about?*
- *The Giant's Causeway was formed how many years ago?*
- *What is Skara Brae?*
- *Who led the group of scientists who were the first to "Split The Atom" ?*

- *Films were first shown publicly in the UK in which year?*
- *In which country was Florence Nightingale born?*
- *What was the approximate UK's iron production during the 19th century?*

In response to criticisms, the Home Office published a booklet to help people revise for the test. Unfortunately, the book contained a number of mistakes and howlers, such as the statement that 'Great Britain includes Northern Ireland', when in fact Great Britain is made up of England, Wales and Scotland. It is the United Kingdom that includes Northern Ireland.

The Scottish Association of Teachers of History wrote to the Home Office to point out some of the mistakes. Their president said, "I find the whole thing appalling. It is riddled with errors and it is the most turgid, abysmal piece of writing I have seen in a long time."

Reception in the UK

It's the neighbour who calls me a neighbour and a friend who is my passport. They have helped me to be here in the UK. It's not the legal paper or anything. And it's the people that I work with, the people that I'm affiliated with. This is the general human–to–human relationality that makes you who you've become, whether you're in UK or in Eritrea; anywhere. That's why.

Yusef

I came here and all of my expectations were actually surpassed. The reality was much greater than what I thought the UK was. The people that treated me, it was great: the school, my friends, even the teachers helped me to build my confidence. And basically everyone that I met in the UK actually helped me to improve who I am and to be proud of who I am and about the journey that I've been through. So yeah, I'm really happy here.

Yezda

I always say British people they are the good. And they are the best in the world. Because the help I have here, I never have it in my life. I always say that. I always say that. Because I have help here and I have peace here.

Haddy

But what I like it here especially, is when there is the ice cream car. I adore it! The man that, when he know that, from the first time: five of us go down and eat. If you see it? He doesn't move until we go and buy the ice cream from him! So from the first time I have a nice feeling from here in the UK.

June

A lot of people don't have an understanding of immigrants, what we go through, and what we struggle, and yet we still make it, we still work hard and still adjust and assimilate. And we still contribute to others. And that's lost in our struggle. And I really want to give voice to what we go through to paint a different picture.

Zula (Eritrea)

Is depend. Sometime it's hard when people ask me, "Where are you from, are you a refugee or asylum seeker?" Is making me feel like sad because I'm a refugee.

No really, sometimes when I have to have something and I asked for it and they didn't do for me, I need it and I feel that, yeah, because I'm a refugee maybe, [they] ignore me.

Daryan

I think word "immigrant" itself makes people think that once you're an immigrant, you're coming here, you are either an asylum seeker, failed asylum seeker or you are a refugee. Why can't it be called expatriates? Yes, that's the word I'm looking for. Why can foreigners be called expatriates? Because that looks like a decent enough word. Then you have respect. Because once you are an "immigrant", then you are an asylum seeker, you are a refugee or anything that is bad.

Rose

The word "refugee" cuts you out.

And it makes you feel like you are being categorised in the element of being a little bit subhuman. Or you have something about you that is not fully human enough, that you have to be labelled refugee for you to be brought into society, brought into that space of being human.

And I never know when being refugee stops. When you win your asylum case and you are being given a status? Or during that period when you're given a status, you have to be refugee until you become a British citizen?

It makes a lot of people that I know who are refugees uncomfortable to be called refugee. Sometimes it seems like you are being prevented from moving forward in society. Because you're a refugee.

Oba

It's a passion of mine to understand how you can be an immigrant in the Western world, because I come from Africa, and our experience as immigrants from developing nations is quite different. When you come to the Western world, it's completely different: the way we understand ourselves, the way we understand others, the way we understand everything! And it's was quite challenging for me when I moved here, even though I spoke English, and I had a lot of experience, I had worked for international NGOs, and I had worked for UN, so I was quite confident that it was going to go good for me in this new world. But quite the contrary- I had a hard time adjusting and understanding the culture. And at that point, I was just hitting my head into walls wherever I go, because there was this lack of understanding of the culture, and also the system and the way people talk, even though I spoke the language, the norm and the value of the culture that's embedded inside, like you cannot see, was very puzzling to me [...] I couldn't even see where I was emotionally, mentally, or in every area of my life, I didn't know where I was. It felt like being thrown in an ocean without a vest.

Zula

If being British is completely unbecoming Eritrean, if being British is completely losing my language, my identity, my culture, my way of being, my food, and everything that I have become since when I was born, that, to me, is not *becoming* something; that, to me, is *unbecoming* what I have been since when I was born.

And that's what I wanted to challenge in my becoming British at the same time. Like, Eritrea is always in a permanent nearness to me. I can't just escape Eritrea, I have my family there, I have my parents there, I have my siblings there, I have lots of cousins there! So that, to me, it is not a different thing. So I do not want to pick my becoming Britishness to dominate my being Eritrean. But I wanted to measure this and create a kind of a perfect attainment between these two identities, where I become a globallly transnational and national citizen at the same time.

Yusef

It transforms your identity, and that's what I was trying to say, that you are not even being seen as an Afghan, or Nigerian, anymore. You are being seen as a refugee.

In relation to what? I don't understand it.

And it makes you feel like your identity has been devalued, and your identity has been reconfigured. Not just reconfigured, because the history that you have about your life; where you come from; the culture; and everything that you come with as a holistic baggage that makes you; it reduces all of that into being a refugee.

It takes your identity away, because as a refugee, if you are seeking asylum, you cannot really go back to the country where you come from. It's like you have to leave everything that you have in that country- your parents, your family, your extended family, you can't go to back to them. And you can only see them if you go to another country and if you meet up in another country.

Some people do not really want to give up the idea of, say for instance, being Nigerian, because that gives you an identity of an origin. But "refugee" cut off that origin, that identity of origin that you had, and you have to start building up your life here, or wherever you find yourself, but finding yourself you have to be labelled "refugee", not as a qualified citizen of that country, until you become one when they give you the country's passport or something like that.

But do you still carry on being refugee?

Oba

208

We talked about in the beginning, the four survivor skills: you have a job, you have a few friends here and there, you can tell your hardship, and you can support each other, and then you have housing situation, and then also the language skills.

Once you have integrated that, it should pull you out from that Survival Mode, right? You're not just living to pay your bills. Life is more than that, right?

So in order to get there, you need to go out of that mentality; you have to get out of the Survival Mode of just repeating the same thing again, and again, and again, and again. Which would mean you have to recognise yourself as a leader, right? Because it would be you making a difference for others, you have to go beyond what you're doing just for you.

Because as immigrants, especially refugees, who have done everything to come to another country: you have no idea the bravery that takes, the courage that takes. They are brave, they are courageous, they are amazing human beings more than they could realise, because now the mind gets stuck in the Survival Mode: "Oh my god, I'm in a new country, oh my God, I have to do this, I have to pay my bills, and then I have to send to my family." And then they're in this spiral, all the time.

I have met people who have been here for thirty years who are still in that mentality, and they have not integrated to the culture fully. They're still in their little bubble in their community. Some of them they don't even speak enough English to get them a job or anything like that, because they work in their small community where they can speak their language. So they have created a very small world.

What refugees and immigrants alike, when you go through something like that, that means you have a greater potential. That means once you have mastered that, now you have to survive in both worlds.

Zula

Your origin, your native, you leave that all of that behind. You can try to recreate it here. But you cannot be in touch with the origin.

Oba

I am a refugee myself, and I've gone through the system, and I know it. And of course, when I came here, I had to hit the ground running, I had to learn the law, the language, and the history.

Idris

The biggest problem I find for asylum seekers and refugees and immigrants in the UK, especially for asylum seekers, is living a life of uncertainty. You don't know where you are going, you don't know what they are going to decide. Because it looks like the Home Office is taking all the time seeing asylum seekers as liars. And the society at large views asylum seekers, immigrants and refugees as people who've come to take their houses, their homes, their schools.

I'll give you an example. The other day I went into the British Heart Foundation charity shop, and when I was there, these two ladies were discussing about school place. And this other old lady says, "The main problem here is these people who've come into our country and taking all the places". You know, you are in there; it makes you feel so bad, I felt so bad. I was the only black person in the there, and you know inwardly that you are an asylum seeker, you know your situation, you know your position, and you feel bad and you think, this is how people look at us, like people just come to take their things, their homes, their school places and all, but we are human beings as well. We are faced with a situation where we cannot help the situation we are in at the moment. And we expect everybody to look at us as human beings and accept us as we are.

Rose

I feel I'm not a European culture inside. I am an "at the back" person. Shy. I don't know how to talk, how to make fast friendship. I don't know this. My friendship come very slowly. Because it is part of our culture.

When I was in University, my principal and the Dean came to a meeting with me, they said, "You are very quiet. You don't talk with anyone."

And I told this is our culture- women should not talk too much. Which women talk too much they're not good women as recognisable.

And my teacher says, "Your work is such a strong, and as a person when I see you, you're not that same person. Your drawing is such a good drawing. No one can tell you do that drawing."

So I feel like all these whatever I learned from my country, my culture, everything is the opposite here. I feel like I'm walking with this hand, my feet is up, and that whole things is up upside down.

Kajoli

The first thing that I felt when I came here was: I looked at these people and they looked giant to me, because I'm like, five foot tall! And they were tall, and they spoke really fast. I told you that I understood English. I even taught English as a second language before I got here. But I couldn't understand the words they were saying because they were talking too fast. Is that English? What are they saying?

And it seems like, they knew everything about everything. Like, as if they were doctors, they had this knowledge that I couldn't comprehend.

So what I felt was like, I felt very small. I felt myself like, shrinking. Like, oh my God, I know nothing, I don't know anything, I don't know if I can survive here.

And it's very normal to feel that way. I am sharing this because that's the most common feeling that people feel when they come to the Western world. You guys are very intimidating!

Zula

It was a little bit challenging when I come over here. In my country we speak English but there is some few words you can't use it here. Like, in my country, if you go are going for a shower, we use "I'm going to bathe." As when I come here and say bathe, they say "What are you going to do? You're going to for shower?"

And the other thing in my country is when you are calling names, like for example, if I want to call your name, here I just call your name straightaway. But in my country, I need to put like "Mr" or, you used to wait to put in "Mr." But here, when you come here, you call someone straight name "Oh, Mark, Mark", or "Steve, Steve" without any "Mr" and the person who doesn't feel like you insulted him, he just feel like it's okay. But someone in my country if you call "Paul": how can you call him Paul?

"You don't put my name? Well, you don't give me respect."

You need to be like, "Oh, Mr. Paul, how are you today?" You know, but here you can say "Oh, hello, Paul. Are you okay?"

"Okay. Yeah, I'm fine."

Or in my country, every time like someone's older than you, when you give her something, like you bring a cup of tea or water? You need to kneel down! Like, "Oh, this is your cup of tea, or water." But here you just bring some cup of tea and "OK, hello, Paul. There you go- your tea." Without anything like that. It was challenging to me, like okay, that's the kind of culture now I'm in.

Paul

I'm just gonna say that one of my culture shock was we, as Africans, we welcome the rain, and we dance in the rain.

And then in the Western world, you even have a song about- "Rain, rain go away, come again another day!"

Zula

Before I wasn't realised what is feminism. I don't know what is feminism. In our culture we didn't learn it. But I learned here what is a feminist.

Kajoli

How do I deal with racism? Like, I was born in Africa, and my colour was never an issue for me before I left Eritrea. And all of a sudden, my colour was discussed, or my colour was an issue, and it gets in the way. So I literally don't know how to handle that because I never seen myself being a problem because of my colour.

So those are things that we need to deal with, but without self-confidence, how are you going to deal with that? Right? I have to be able to stand before other people and be equal. How am I going to do that if I don't feel confident?

Zula

I no longer have a single answer to "what is home". Maybe the younger version of me might have thought it was a physical place. The version of me today thinks it's a spiritual place. It's a place of being, which is home.

This idea aligns with a lot of Sufi traditions, you know, that if you find hardship in one area of the world, that you should actually move on and find peace somewhere else, because at the end of the day, the whole world is God's land anyway. And if you look at the big picture, really: eighty years, a hundred years, five hundred years in the scope of human history and the world history? It's not even a blip! So if you look at the big picture, life becomes much easier. And the goal becomes more clear. So we need to remind folks out there it is most likely that whoever's pushing against refugees, their ancestors might have gone under the same xenophobia, just a couple of clicks back.

Mo

Brexit was run on the racist vote. I will call it a racist vote. Because the government they confuse all the people. They say these asylum seekers, the gay here or the European people, come here and they take all your money, they take all your NHS. But they see people they come in work and earn their money. They don't take anyone's job, but it's the politician make the people think that we have more jobs or more care in the NHS but it has actually gone worse, so that's why they're in a situation of confusion now.

So you're not getting drugs- because there's no doctors in the hospitals.

Can we stay in the single market? They already knew that it's not going to work for Britain if they are not in a single market. But why did they introduce the referendum? That was a racist war.

August

Asylum seekers and refugees should not be blamed for every political problem. Because every time there's a problem, they blame it on asylum or refugees. So people should take account of their own problems and not just blame it on asylum seekers or refugees as well.

Rose

Everywhere the media is the extension of the government. And it's the media that does the job to make the people's mind-set. And the media is full of anti-refugee propaganda. There are lots of writing *against* refugees and nothing *by* refugees.

Yasmin

My problem is that asylum seekers are seen as uneducated people. But behind our background, we are educated and we can actually contribute to the society. If we're given an opportunity to do it, we can show the world that we can actually give something to the society.

Rose

When I go to a university setting and talk about my life I realise that the professors are astonished to see that we have crystal chandeliers in my house. They are astonished to see that we have Victorian furniture or, or... what did you actually think about us before you met us?

Mo

I think the problem of being a refugee or an asylum seeker is that the British people view you as you are somebody who has come to get something out of the country, somebody who has come to get and not give. So we are looked at as somebody who has come to get the riches, get the jobs, fill schools for the children. Everything that is bad is blamed on asylum seekers and refugees.

Rose

When I was naïve and young I always thought that like, oh, why would the world treat us any different? At the end of the day, we're very similar.

Well, to my surprise [laughs]...

To any immigrant's surprise, the world does not see us as equals.

So, as, simple as it sounded in my brain, I continuously am surprised and astonished how much of this is new information to many people.

Mo

The economic situation is worse than before. In the past we wouldn't see this much homeless that we see now. And the governments need a scapegoat for these economic problems that they don't want to address. They don't want to help people. So they need scapegoats.

They blame refugees for all these problems.

Yasmin

It took four years before they accept me to stay in the country. And that was again another really little bit disappointment. But I enjoyed the generosity of people who are involved in volunteering and supporting. And you know, you compare all that goodness versus the system. I started kind of rationalising it, to know that I'm not being mistreated by people: I'm being mistreated by the system.

Aston

You know, like, if we came here and we didn't find your organisation [Refugee Radio], we are really, like, we'll be in more bad situation, because they just put us in a house and you have to wait and they didn't ask what we are feeling and what we go through before that. It's like, okay we arrived here, they think we are okay, very happy and we are not really. I didn't come here like: okay I'm in the UK I have a room, even if the room is small, but really if they give me a five stars hotel I don't want that! I just I need to feel comfortable. I need to feel like support from people because I didn't come a full person. I come a broke person to this country.

Saleh

Prisoners of Conscience is an organisation based in the UK, in London, and they are working with the people, particularly of my background, refugees, migrants, human rights defenders who have run away for one reason or another. And the thing that we have in common is that one way or another, we have been imprisoned or we are prisoners of conscience, not because of doing something that is criminal, but because of taking a stand for the rights of others. And they're doing a phenomenal job. They are very wonderful people. They're fantastic. They have taken time and again, to check on me how I'm doing, asking or of course, is there anything we can do? Apart from giving me bursaries again, and again, and again, they have not gotten tired of always asking, okay, is there anything that we can do? Sometimes I'm sitting here on my desk, and then I see mail come in, and they're like, oh, there is this opportunity? Or there is this? Can you take a look at it? And this is one of the things that they do. And I think they're doing a wonderful job, they give hope to people who are hopeless.

When I joined Leicester University, I didn't have the money that was required of me. But right from the beginning, they [Prisoners of Conscience] have always been there, paying the school fees, giving me bursaries when I needed, giving me guidance when I need it, and of course, telling me look this way, look this way, try this, try this. So they are always there with guidance and of course, material help. Like sometimes they also give, maybe you don't know, like a hardship allowance. If you are in a hardship, especially after arriving in a new country, you don't have anywhere else to turn, and you turn to them. They don't say no. And they don't ask questions that they don't need to ask, of course, they are required to ask but they don't ask certain things. They see the need; they chip in when you are in need. And then other matters, they follow up later. So I think it is a very wonderful thing they're doing.

Idris

In the five years I am here, the first time I lived with my son.

The second time, I lived in the hotel from the council.

The third time, I went to a faraway county.

And the fourth thing, I came live with that lady.

The fifth time, I live in emergency accommodation in a place which is full of drugs-people, homeless people, nasty people. I remember there is a police come to the home and I thought it is a delivery coming bringing something. But when I saw that it was the police I said, I didn't do anything wrong!

The police he start laughing. He told me, "It is not you. Did you hear any argue in front of your flat?"

I told him no, because when I lock the inside door I cannot hear what is in the building. But I can still hear what is in the street. So I understand from the neighbours, I know that the one downstairs he is a dealer. Oh my god, and there is a lot of people. I don't know the drug, the smoking how it is, but the smell… when I'm entered into the flat I found that there is a bad smell, which I am not getting used to it. And all the time I'm having a bad headache! I think from what I'm smelling from them. Sometimes they come from the outside near my window from the street there, because I'm in the first floor, and at least I got my permanent home now.

I moved to sheltered accommodation. This is what I was looking for it.

Why? Because my health it is not good.

June

221

I don't know who it was, but they're sending me message, called me first and say, "You're gonna move on".

I said, where?

They said, "We doesn't know yet, but somebody who will pick you up, he knows." They say, "You have to pack all of your stuff."

The thing that is getting me feel okay a little bit was when I ask the driver, where we going to?

He say "We're going to Paddington." But he mean we're going to Brighton! I was thinking he was saying, "We're going to Paddington."

So I say, yeah, that's good, that's good.

But when I first saw the city of Brighton, I don't like it! I got sad again and I stay away from the people again. So they get me to the house, I find somebody in the house, I said, how are you? I was thinking he was manager of the house, but he was somebody like me, he moved today. And after that another guy moved, that was all the people. One was forty-five, another one is fifty, and I'm the youngest one.

So yeah, I moved to this house and I don't know anybody, just sad. I got a lot of depression for four months. And after that I start to go out again, walk to the beach, walk to the city. So and after that I love it! I love Brighton. So it was quite nice, and it's nice now, but, when I moved here, I was really upset and doesn't like this city, because I didn't know anybody. And this is my problem: I don't like to move around and to meet new people.

Mostafa

Brighton is a free city. Everyone can be whatever she want to be. It is different to other places- there is nobody can give you bad looks, wherever you are. And there is a lot of activities in Brighton for adults, children and teenagers as well. And there is the sea, the beach. As me, I like cycling a lot, so Brighton is friendly for bike, like when you cycle, because there is a lot of bikes, so there is a lot of respect for cycles, so they'll be good for me and for them, because normally I take even my daughter here and we used to cycle together, so I can't wait for that, even now I could go cycling with my two daughters following me, or follow them, guiding them. So Brighton is good. There is a lot of activities in Brighton.

According to the other places I've been living, like Manchester, I was there but I was isolated. Even I wouldn't understand them. They speak English, but different one. So I was struggling when I was in Manchester, going to buying things and I didn't understand, and they speaks all the same. But when I come to Brighton I feel like, okay.

Paul

I love Brighton because nobody cares about anybody. You walk by yourself, nobody asking what you're doing. And I like Refugee Radio, that's nice things; talk to people, that's nice. We're all friends. Most of the people who comes here to Refugee Radio, I also see them outside. I love to come here every week, it's really nice.

Mostafa

And at that time, I was so happy to know the Refugee Radio people, which they helped me so much. The first time I was living with my son from the time I come here almost for seven months. And after that the council, as I become a homeless, they put me in a hotel for one and a half months. And after that I cannot stay more than that, because I don't have any paper. I didn't get my status. So the Refugee Radio people, they helped me by finding me a place with the family. I have to go to them. And they are really, really nice people, helping me by myself so much.

June

I love you guys so much. I will never forget you in my life. And I will never forget MindOut in my life [mental–health charity for LGBTQ community]. They done a lot for me, MindOut. I love them. And I love you guys. Especially Emma. I love Emma.

Because at that time, if you didn't have patience then you would never have helped me. Because my brain is not working. I always say rubbish things, because of my trauma. And when they bring me here, I do worse and worse than that. You people have been patient with me. Even if I say something bad, you didn't even say to me, "Look, don't come to us anymore." Especially when I applied my papers to the lawyer to claim asylum, it is made me mad. I always talk. But you people have patience to me. So I just want to say thank you Steve, thank you Gemma [Refugee Radio]. Definitely. I'm so happy for you guys.

Haddy

And of course at that time, every week they're having a meeting with us [Refugee Radio mental-health support group], which is helped us mentally. I was so shy to talk with anyone, especially to tell them my problems. When I start telling anyone about anything, I started crying! I said, why I'm crying? I have to get used that I'm going to be refused. And I'll make another fresh claim, another something which is it will help me, but what is inside me still…

So I tried to go to the meeting every week, which is helping when I find the people. I told the lady there, "Don't ask me to talk in front of the people. If you want to know my problem, I'll tell it to you by ourselves, me and you."

And suddenly I found that the people they're nice, everyone there is telling their problem. And I start talking. And I find that when everyone find me telling them my problems, they start talking as well. I encourage them to take everything they have it inside and talk.

Until now they are helping us. Really they are a helpful people. The manager there, Mister Steve, and the two nice ladies there, they are so clever, they're so helpful. And even sometimes they are taking us as an activities [Refugee Radio walking group] to go in the gardens outside, which is helped us so much not to feel scared from anything. And from that time we feel that we are like a family.

And they introduce us to another community which is helping us, called 1000 For One Thousand (T4K). Mister Jacob also he is so helpful. Mister Steve introduced us to him just to solve our problems about my status. And we become as a friends. We have to see each other every week. If I didn't come they will call me: "What is the matter with you?"

June

Reception in the UK– Notes

Many of our respondents speak highly of Brighton and of how welcoming they have found it. In terms of identifying with their new home, it is possible that the idea of Brighton is more important to them than the idea of Britain, especially for those who were dispersed around the country as asylum seekers and those who experienced discrimination or racism elsewhere.

Refugees experience racism differently from second or third generation immigrants. Our respondent, Zula, makes the point that, "My colour was never an issue for me before I left." She did not feel that she was a person of colour until she felt like she was the only person of colour.

One theme that came up repeatedly was the role of the voluntary sector in making people welcome and facilitating their new lives. Besides Refugee Radio, there were three other charities that came up in the interviews:

Thousand 4 £1000, or T4K as they are known, are a local charity who seek to create a 'Hospitable Environment' by disrupting the immigration policies that force people onto the streets. Their main activity is crowdfunding flats in Brighton to house destitute asylum seekers who would otherwise be forbidden from renting. They are entirely run by volunteers and are spearheaded by Jacob Berkson, who was interviewed in Castaway Heritage (2019) about his life and work.

MindOut is a mental-health charity run by and for LGBTQ people in Brighton and Hove. They provide advice and advocacy as well as peer support groups, mentoring and counselling. Their recent report, (Pathways Between LGBTQ Migration, Social Isolation and Distress, 2022), described how liberating migrants found living in a city with a high number of LGBTQ people, how they felt safer, and how their experiences of the place shaped their mental health, "particularly their healing experiences of Brighton's green and blue spaces". They found that migrants were disappointed to suffer exclusion in the city, however, when it came to their mental health.

Prisoners of Conscience are a London-based charity who have been running since 1962. In that time, they have provided practical and financial help to over 10,000 political prisoners. Their resettlement work includes offering bursaries so that refugees can access qualifications- in many cases this means people requalifying so that they can continue to work in their original professional field, as the UK does not recognise most foreign qualifications. Without this kind of support, it would be impossible to start all over again and people would lose the professional identities that other migrants rely upon. Too often, refugees who were previously lawyers, teachers and doctors in their home countries find themselves unemployed or underemployed in the UK.

PTSD

If you are deemed insane in my country, they just take you to an asylum or take you to a psychiatric ward. And there is two types– there is the one that is run by the herbalist, and that one is more brutal because they chain people and they beat them up, they give them concussion. And the government one, you're just locked away from society.

If I know of a woman who has a mental health problem in our community and they decide she is a functioning person, but has a mental problem, the society will just try to stay away from her even though she is trying to survive with children. She prepared this thing called *fufu* [West African dough] and she sell it to the people. People buy from her, but people don't interact with her. They only interact with her from the support they give her through the sales of the *fufu*. Nobody asks her how she is doing, or how she's struggling, or something like that. And if she run amok for instance, the government will pick her up, or the family members will pick her up and put her in the ambulance to the psychiatric ward.

Trauma is not something that is spoken about. I didn't even know the trauma really existed.

Oba

In my home country, some people is shy talking about the mental health. Because some people thinking: if talking about mental health, the thinking about him is bad and maybe some people scared and say, "This guy's crazy," or something like that. In my country some people doesn't want to talk about it.

When I came to England, I didn't have anything like this one, but after like three or four months is happen for me. Is like depression, I couldn't sleep. And after that, I've found it out that, for me, I have depression and anxiety.

I was shy talking about that. And I didn't feel comfortable. But after this, I went to a GP and I explained. I said, I can't sleep, and they referred me to Wellbeing [NHS mental-health service]. And they say to me after that I had to talk about the mental health.

I'm talking about the mental health; it was new for me.

Daryan

When I was a girl, I avoid going outside because people rape me or something. So I remain in the house.

That's why I'm scared of people. Very, very scared of people. The flat I am living in now, I am scared of the man who lives opposite me. He got mental health problems and is shouting day, night, anytime. It's not safe for me at all. Shouting every night, day and night. He bangs my door. Our doors are opposite.

Haddy

Do I am a crazy woman? This is what we have within our mind in our country. If you go to the mental health, that means you are a crazy, you are not a normal person.

So when I met the therapist, she start talking to me as if she is living with me. And she discovered that I'm having PTSD. Yes, I feel it, but I don't know what is it exactly. So she start to meet us and she referred me to a hospital place somewhere out from here. And at that time, because of what had happened at the Home Office, when I went to that doctor, I start crying and screaming I'm so scared. For example, like a police car, or ambulance car, which is scaring me so much, even any noise in front of me: I shout. So I explained for her what had happened at the Home Office. And at once she wrote a letter to the Home Office. And I talked to my GP about what had happened, which is affect my PTSD. And they send it to the Home Office.

Next time when I'm going for the reporting, they change three hundred and sixty degree. They treat me very nice. "You can have a seat." Because I'm having a problem using a walker. So: "You have a seat here," or, "No, give her the way! You sit here, let her go first!" So what is the reason? Because of what the GP and the doctor complain about, the Home Office, they start treating us better.

And I stay with that lady for almost three years. Which like we become a family. She can know me from my eyes.

June

I think that pain is not go in my life because it's all over my body. Especially the rape and what I am going through, from when I was young until I grow up. I think that pain is with me for life. I didn't know how to take that off to my system. But I do know it's not going to happen.

I will never forget the rape and the forced marriage and what I am going through when I was young. It's not easy at all to go through that. And I didn't see my mum. At that time I need my mum. But she is not there for me. I blame her and don't blame her, because at that time she's there to work to buy some food for the house.

Sometimes I say when she is going she have to take me there. Better than leaving me with my aunties. And they use me all the time. I'll never forget it.

Then my mother come back from the village and married again. And after that I lived with my stepdad. It was worse. When I take showers he always turns off the tap, all of the water. He says my dad is not paying the water. He don't allow me to use the water to take shower. It's not easy at all.

That stepdad is a very bad person. Because when we eat, because we eat together, if I tried to eat some of the meat, he won't allow me to touch it, because it's not my father's money. And it's very hard for me.

Because the food he buy is for his children. It is not for me. And the water is not for me. I go through all that. That's why sometimes if I angry or my brain is not good then I always talk, talk, talk, without stop. If I angry a little bit, is make me remember all this thing. So I always talk, talk, talk, talk. This makes me very, very, very, angry. I can cope if I am angry.

If anytime I wake up, anger is come to me. I always remember what I passed through and I asked myself, why that happened to me?

Haddy

I was talking to someone about this the other day. It's funny you mentioned it, because the only time in my country that you actually think about going to get professional help, is if you have gone crazy, literally. And the only hospital that we have for mental health is in the capital city. It's called, well… the closest translation is, "for people who are crazy".

Zula

face. And it is not easy that I forget all this thing in one time. But you see us, I'm trying to be always a positive lady. Try to think about the good thing not about the bad thing. Everybody see me they're thinking that I don't have any problem in my life. Because all the time I'm going smiling. Even my health it is not in a good way. And I don't know what to say. But at least I'm happy that sometimes when you take what is inside you, take that bad thing and put it outside of you, you feel relaxed.

But relax, it will not be at the same time.

Don't worry, I'm going to take my tabs [tablets] and try to sleep, because yesterday I couldn't sleep at all. I slept only two hours. What is the reason for that, I don't know.

June

I suffered a lot of mental, physical, psychological torture. I have a lot of nightmares as a result of what I've been through. And, as you can see on my body, I have a lot of scars.

If you see my body, here, these are some of these scars that I got. I was tortured. I live with that. We were detained in the prison for ten months. Because of the belief we have, that our people need to be free. Because of the innermost torture that I face in Cameroon. I have had a lot of post-traumatic stress as a result of that.

If I'm speaking today, I think I will thank God,

because at one time, during one of my arrest and detention, I felt I was gonna die because of the torture inflicted on me. I never knew I could exist. I never knew that I was going to be alive. But by the sheer intervention of God, I was able to survive. Because we were not given any medical attention. I've showed you the scars I've got all over my body, the injuries, nobody did anything about it. I basically survive by the intervention of God. So I have a lot of nightmares, a lot of bad memories as to what I've been through. To be molested because of my belief is cowardly.

So these are things that has actually affected my life.

Sometimes I wake up at night and I feel I have a nightmare where I see them rushing after me. You know, some of them from the secret service, they used to wear all green. So particularly if I see somebody wearing a green shirt, I become frightened. I become paranoid. Because I have the feeling that, oh, look out, the agents are coming again for me.

Sometimes, when I see the police, or I see the word "police", I'm frightened because of the way I've been tortured in Cameroon by the secret police. So this is what I've got to deal with. Day in, day out.

I'm still spreading the history, the literature of Southern Cameroon. And I am not going to give up this struggle. I'm not going to be frightened by the fact that we have been subjugated by the Government of the Republic. We will do all what we can do.

John

If they really believe us, or they really sent a professional person from the NHS like to listen to us, or to understand what we need, or what we felt from inside- not just, "Okay, I'm in good health," or, "You look like a good health."

So unfortunately I was not like that.

If you just speak with me one word, you will hear a million words back. Because we need to talk. We need to someone to listen to us.

Saleh

I can't say I didn't have help. I have, but it's not enough, I think.

Some doctor is listen to you, and they give you the time to understand. But some doctor? No, just they give you this medicine.

It's better if we could have more time. Because sometimes, I have appointment and I should talk about another things. When you called for appointment, they ask you, what is your issue? You know, what is your problem? And you said, okay, I have eye pain problem, and when you're going to appointment, I have another problem, I needed to talk about that. The doctor doesn't give you the time.

I had an appointment about my back problem and I went, and I needed to talk about my mental health, and another health condition, but they didn't let me talk. They said, "Yeah, our time is finished and you don't have more time. You should make it another appointment for talking about mental health and knee."

And I ignored it. I didn't call back. Because I really, I don't like it.

Daryan

I've been told many times that GPs have, like, ten minutes to talk to patients when they go to see them. But when you are a refugee and asylum seeker, you have lots on your mind! You have your immigration case, you have your trauma, you have your culture-shock, you have isolation, and homelessness, and all these things that are compounding your health problem. And you need to be listened to, to be understood, as well as being supported in an holistic manner to help you resolve your mental health problem.

Oba

I have the problem in my back pain.

And I went to the GP, like, too many time, and just they give me the medicine and I talking about them my sleeping, because I couldn't sleep. I had trauma. And they referred me after to the Wellbeing [primary mental health services] and I had one appointment with interpreter and it was take one hour. They asked me the question and, after this appointment, I didn't get any appointment.

And just I tried going to the GP talking about that.

After that, Refugee Radio they find for me someone to help about the my sleeping and trauma. I had every Tuesday go to see their own person.

Daryan

I was at the crisis point. I was already self-harming. I was overdosing on medication, which is also harming my physical health, because I have a liver problem and taking overdose is impacting on the liver, and I was snowballing into catastrophe.

My friends really did a lot of work in terms of helping me to contact different organisations, understand mental health, to come with me, to come to talk to my GP, and to understand the gravity of my state of health.

Oba

It was like three years. Yeah, three years I couldn't sleep. Some night even I couldn't sleep one hour, and I use it work this time.

When I went to my job the people asked me: "Why you look like that? You look tired."

And it was hard for me to explain to them...

Daryan

When I was in Swansea, I think my trauma was becoming evidential. And a friend told me that I have to speak to someone about it. I went to engage with the mental health services in Swansea. And I was made to see a psychologist, or psychiatrist, I can't remember.

I told him: I've lost two of my siblings within three months, to the same type of illness which I'm suffering from. I have an ongoing immigration issue, and I told them how that affects me, and things like that.

And then they told me, he was like, "Oh, you will be fine, because your problem is just a social problem. And when you resolve your immigration case, everything is gonna sort itself out."

And I just feel they denied the fact that I have trauma, bereavement and all those other issues that is, you know, weighing down on me. They did not even investigate if this mental health that I'm experiencing is the protracted issue, which I have been having.

Looking back now, I had this issue since I was child, but he didn't even go there.

He just told me, "You will be fine if you resolve your immigration issue."

Oba

It's too hard for me talk on the phone. I prefer to face-to-face because it's better and the doctor can see me. But when you have an appointment on the phone,

243

make you feel maybe sad or depressed.

In my case, looking back now, and having been to therapy, some symptoms of mental health did occur in my childhood, where every evening I felt very sad, like, not just sad, like deep sadness. I don't know why. And that swings in the morning and I feel better, and that kind of thing. And other stuff happened in my

Being left without help is make me feel down and day by day I get the worse. My problem is getting worse day by day.

Daryan

The Home Office, when they interviewed you, there is a culture of not believing you. They make you

childhood that made me feel very worthless, because I felt like I have to strive very hard to prove myself in society even though I was a child.

Oba

I didn't find that the government or Home Office or NHS like to make me feel I'm a human. Just I found the support from other different organisations [refugee charities] and I'm looking for a safe place. I'm looking for a safe health. I'm looking for a good health. I'm looking for good support for health.

Saleh

I did not understand trauma or PTSD before I came to the UK. No, like I was saying, even if you've been through an ordeal you are not considered of having been through some significant emotional or mental health problem, you just seen as being through a hard time. You get over it. You just move on to the next thing.

Oba

Since I arrived to Brighton I was thinking: what I have to do? What I'm doing here? What I will wait for, day-by-day? And it's getting to be a bad situation. So I started to call a GP and I asked them can I get a psychological therapy?

And the person who answered the phone he said, "Why you need psychology?

I said, I need the psychology because I'm tired, I feel I'm not okay, I feel bad.

He said, "Why? What you need?"

I said, um, I need that, I need the doctor. And he made a phone call to another line or something like that and it's like no one believes you, or if you need support from psychology or from GP, then they will not believe you, even if they saw you in the floor, or even if they saw you hurt yourself.

When I'm being in a bad situation, like being like more worse, more worse, till I hurt myself. Who need to hurt himself or who need who to hurt herself? No one needs that. Everybody loves our body or ourselves. We need to live our life. If I hate my body then I will stay in my country! I saw many of bad story or many of bad days in my country, but I came here, I'm looking for a safe place, I'm looking for a safe health, I'm looking for a good health, I'm looking for good support for health. They didn't answer me. They didn't believe me in the beginning until I started to hurt myself and that was out of my control: because a lot of thinking in my mind. I was overdoing thinking, I was thinking a lot, worried, waiting, that's not easy.

Even if you saw me and my body in good health, you can't see inside. It's like we all are looking for someone to feel what we feel from inside, not from outside.

If I am look like a good person, or like a healthy man, but from inside like I really suffering, so how I can explain that and no one come to listen to me? From the GP or from the hospital, no one come to listen to me. So it was like they thought they just can help us with the medication.

The medication doesn't help. What helps is when you come to listen. When you come to really feel like, yeah, I found people they support me, I found that support from people, from organisations who are not working with the NHS. They are working with a charity, or they are volunteering. I found support from them. They come to me, they come to listen to me, they come to give me a positive words, to make me feel- yeah, I'm not alone here.

I came here, I come from different country, I have no anything. Like, how to say? It was like I was born in new here in the UK. But, with a lot of, a lot of, a lot of things in my heart or my mind.

Saleh

I think it is very important to let those people know what the asylum seekers have passed through because some of them can be having some problem like medical condition and they cannot attend to the GP because they are asylum seekers and I think this is not right. It is not right because when you are an asylum seeker and have some problem like medical, I think you need to have some treatment, but some of them, you can go there and they say, because you don't have paper, you are not entitled.

So you can suffer and it can even make your mental health to become worse because you look like you don't have anywhere to go because of your status and even you can go with depression and stress and after you can have mental.

Paul

And if you go to the GP and tell them, they give you only medicine. And they are not referring you to the mental health.

The medicine I am taking, I told them it just make me worse at night. I have nightmare, flashback and I woke up screaming. From the medicine, I just woke up with a bad headache. When I woke up, I found myself my tears are coming down.

June

I think, for me, there is a culture of not believing asylum seekers or refugees. When you go to them and you said to them that you are experiencing something like this, or something like this happened to you, they just think your situation is social circumstances that just need your immigration to be resolved, or even they don't believe you that you are going through that. They don't even believe your story. They don't believe that you are going through such thing, as if mental health cannot happen to an asylum seeker or refugee.

I would want them to understand that there is a pre-migratory condition that cause mental health, like when war happen in the country, or you have broken from the family ties and you are forced to leave, or you are persecuted and you are forced to flee and go into exile, all these things build up mental health.

Like, in my case, I didn't know I had a mental health problem before, when I was a child. Looking back now, I can see some patterns that point to mental health issues, but there was no mental health support in my country. You are either mad or you are sane.

Oba

This is what the people think about mental health: that they are a crazy people, a mad people, so this is their style like that, nobody could treat them.

June

There is also post-migratory problem, like when you are trying to do your asylum process and you are going to places and they keep telling you, "No." If you need housing they tell you, "No."

You couldn't provide food for yourself. You couldn't contribute to the society. You couldn't do all those things. You couldn't have a hope. You couldn't have the ambition to do things for yourself. All these things build up and become the mental health problem.

They think that you are just an alien. You are not a human being. They don't take you seriously.

Oba

I passed through a lot, like torture, all that stuff, and it affects me mentally and physically. And when you go to them to explain, they say, "You don't have paper, so you can't get help."

Like me, my case, I was having mental health, and nobody believes me. There is no anywhere I can run to get some help.

When you try to go somewhere you think you can get help- "Sorry there is nothing we can do because you don't have paper."

So it increases your mental, day and night.

At one time, when I've got a chance and I get some private doctor [via immigration legal aid] so he look at my case and my mental and he try to write a report [medico-legal report as evidence of torture for the asylum claim]. When they write the report that's the time I can get some, a little bit, help.

We need to get some people to raise that case, to have a voice for other refugee people, because I think there is a lot of people in my situation and they don't get help. And they need it.

Paul

My case really pushed me to suicide when people don't believe me. I went to my GP and I told them that this is my situation and he just told me like, "Oh, your problem is just your circumstances. If you sort your immigration out you will just be fine."

And that really offended me. And as from there on and I start harming myself, I started cutting myself, I start taking overdose and doing horrible stuff to myself. I didn't look after myself after that.

Then I moved to Brighton. And still the same thing: doctors were not listening to me. What I'm trying to say is that, when they don't listen to you, or they don't believe you, it translate into another stage in mental health problem, it accumulates and, when it becomes escalated, that is when they start listening to you, when things have already gone bad.

When it is already bad, that's when they listen to you, like when you went to the hospital for overdose.

On top of that, their hands are tied when they find out that you don't have papers. So nowadays, it feels like they want to save you, but the immigration papers that you don't have to be able to access this treatment prevent them from referring you further. So you are still stuck in the same situation. So I'm talking about being an asylum seeker now, not as somebody who has a status. You're in a revolving door, you can't get out of the cycle.

Oba

At that time I had a mental health problem, it was really strong. They moved me from Croydon into a hostel in Manchester [...] but when I went to the GP, the reception people they don't give you the chance.

"Ah, where are you from?"

"I am from Croydon."

"What is your status?"

"I am an asylum seeker but I want to see the doctor because I have some problem."

"Sorry you can't see the doctor unless you sort out your paper, as you are not allowed to be in this country. You cannot have any service, so there is nothing we can do."

So I just stand there in the reception. And at that time didn't know even Steve [Refugee Radio], nobody. I don't know anyone to call to explain the situation to get some help. Or maybe they can call to do this or this [...] so I was stuck. Finally I went back home to where they put us, by myself. That's the time I feel like what am I doing? That's the time I really need to disappear. Yeah, like to take my life away. That's the time I take a lot of tablets.

I wouldn't know myself. Vomiting and this and this. It was really, really horrible- but why? Because you go there to get some help and they refuse, you know.

Paul

GPs or the surgery staff should not be turning away anybody who is an asylum seeker or refugee saying that, "Oh, we are not able to access that particular service." That's against the law. That's my understanding. That's something that should be standard that they should know about.

GPs should know about the NICE clinical guidance with regards to effective treatments for people with complex PTSD. They cannot just be prescribing medication on its own; they need to be thinking about psychological input as well, because the combination of the two actually improves somebody's chances of improving their wellbeing far much better than just prescribing medication.

I know why sometimes the GPs will just prescribe the medication: because most probably they will say, oh, it's about the waiting times, or the waiting list to access that psychological input. But they shouldn't be doing that. They should be trying as best as possible to ensure that somebody is actually accessing psychological input as well.

Samson (Southern Africa)

You're going to have a lot of emotion that comes when you move to a new country, you're going to feel stressed, you're gonna feel a lot of anxiety, a lot of fear, because you don't know the people, you don't know how to do it. And you can be walking around and then, you know, your heart is racing, you don't know what to do with that. You will have a lot of anger because your whole world just shifted, right? There is a lot of emotion that goes within yourself. And if you don't know how to manage it, it will be very difficult to adjust to your new country; you cannot even feel like you belong, because you're always lost in your emotions.

Zula

You have to be friends with the people otherwise you will find yourself sitting depressed, with anxiety, and some people they might hurt themselves when they're sitting alone. Nobody talked with them, just thinking about the bad thing they're having in their life.

June

Taking care of your mental health is very important. I talk about my own experience of mental health. Even though it's a taboo, you don't even talk about it.

Zula

And as you see, I like to make cakes and cookies and something like that which I enjoy it, when I'm doing it, and it make all my depression and anxiety, which is to go out.

June

In the beginning when I came here, everything that goes on in my mind and in my emotion was erratic. Like: "Oh, my God, I need to make money real fast!" And I also left my son behind. So I had to get him here. So there was also a time crunch, right, I had to really run. And the rest of the thing was invisible to me.

And I remember, someone very close to me said, "Oh, my God, you know where you live in the city is very close to the countryside and you know there are places that you can go." And I looked at this person, as if he was crazy, because I was on a mission and he was gonna distract me! And he was talking about, "Oh, you need to go here, you have to go there."

I'm like, are you serious? I am on that Survival Mode and I cannot see anything else.

And after about two years, I met a friend through a friend. He was really a wonderful person. He's a veteran. And we got connected through a common friend who lived in Germany. And then when he spoke about his experience as a soldier and stuff like that, I was like: "Oh my God, how is that possible?"

Everything we were talking about, it was my experience! Because I also went to the military when I was in Eritrea, as a mandatory service.

And I was like: "Oh my God, you grew up here, and I grew up somewhere else, and our experiences are very similar."

So we really became best friends. And then then he said at some point, "Listen- you are stressed a lot.

You're doing a fantastic job, but you need to have a break. You're always on the go, and I understand why you have to do this, but I want to show you a little bit of the places outside of the city."

And I said, "Okay, like, I don't think it's going to make any difference because I really need to go back to work and do the work."

And oh my God! It wasn't even far, and we went to the forest and I... I was mesmerised. It was a very transformative experience for me, because I've never been around trees like that. They're huge. And I was embraced in that nature, and the smell. And I just felt like all the stress, all the anxiety, all the thing that I was feeling, just melted. Like, I couldn't even believe it. And at that point, I actually had this experience where I felt I was not in this country. I was not even in my country. I was not anywhere but just embraced by nature.

And I'm like: why didn't I know about this?

It took me two years to realise that all I needed was to go to nature and to go to the ocean. It's not a warm ocean like Africa or the Mediterranean Ocean, but it's still an ocean and it gives me that sense of you know... whenever I felt overwhelmed, I go there.

So I encourage immigrants to have that experience, to come out of their mentality of, "Oh no, I don't have time for that. Oh no, I can't think about that. I just have to focus on my family and everything that I need to do."

Because you need to relax. If you don't relax, your mind doesn't work. If you don't somehow release the tension and the stress and the anxiety, you are not doing anything anyways, because you're just adding more stress and more frustration to your situation.

It's beautiful to be around nature.

Zula

PTSD- Notes

Post-Traumatic Stress Disorder (PTSD) is an anxiety disorder that can occur when a person has been subject to traumatic experiences. The diagnosis evolved out of earlier war-related concepts such as shell-shock or combat-shock. A separate diagnosis exists called Complex-PTSD, which relates to people who have suffered multiple traumatic experiences over a period of time, such as victims of torture or domestic violence, as these can prove more intractable in treatment. We will use the terms interchangeably for simplicity.

Someone who has PTSD may manifest symptoms like insomnia, nightmares or night-terrors, where they wake up screaming. They will be hypervigilant and can be jumpy, with an exaggerated startle-response and they may go out of their way to avoid places or things that remind them of their trauma. They can feel very stressed all of the time and can struggle to manage feelings of anger or thoughts of suicide. They might experience periods of dissociation where they seem to disconnect and drift away, or even flashbacks, where they feel they are catapulted into the past to relieve traumatic incidents.

This happens because of the way that memories get filed in the brain.

Every time your brain records a memory, it gets filed away in a cabinet with an accompanying emotion. You might remember eating an ice-cream on a nice day, for example, and this image will be stored with the memory of happiness and the sensation of taste. When bad things happen, you might file them away with feelings such as repulsion or fear.

But a problem can arise when the memory is particularly traumatic, especially if your brain tries to file it away with the wrong emotion.

An example of the wrong emotion is the shame or guilt felt by victims of sexual assault. The traumatic experience is not your fault and you should not feel ashamed. But your self-preservation instincts might lead you to blame yourself or take a negative view of your actions as a way to try to learn from the experience and prevent it happening again. And, although this may seem like a helpful survival mechanism, it is still the wrong way to feel about what happened.

So, when this happens, the memory does not fit into the cabinet. It has the wrong label attached to it. It sticks out like a bulky folder and you cannot close the drawer. So instead of becoming a memory, it stays in the front of your mind as if it is an ongoing experience, as if it is happening right now. You remain on red alert, because your brain is telling you that you are still in danger, and over time this becomes increasingly hard to cope with- you cannot relax, you cannot sleep, you cannot even walk down the street without feeling like you are walking through the danger zone. You have one foot in the present and the other foot forever in the worst moment of your life.

Traumatic experiences do not always lead to PTSD, of course. Some of the factors that influence when it might happen include your age at the time, how many times it happened, the support you receive afterwards and the relative degree of control or helplessness you had in the situation.

So why does PTSD get its own chapter?

I started Refugee Radio as a way to help give a voice to people who were voiceless and as a way to help people tell their own stories in their own words. And the stories that I heard came back to PTSD again and again. The refugees and asylum seekers I spoke to told me about their experiences in the past of war, sexual violence, abuse and torture and they told me about the problems they were having coping with their lives today. They told me that they thought about suicide and some of them had tried to kill themselves. I realised that so many of them were struggling with PTSD but they had no formal diagnosis and no treatment whatsoever.

Every now and then I might come across someone who had tried to talk to their GP about the problems they were having. They might get prescribed sleeping tablets or anti-depressants, which have no beneficial impact on PTSD, but the majority received no help at all. Hardly any of them had ever been referred to mental-health services, and those that had been referred were always discharged without help, having been told by the gatekeepers that their problems were purely down to their immigration status and that they should just rely on refugee charities instead.

So, they would go back to their lives, humiliated at having bared their most intimate traumas to a stranger in a clinical setting and then simply being dismissed afterwards. They would never try again. They would spend the rest of their days as the walking wounded, going through the motions, but unable to find any joy or sense of a future for themselves. Just because they were refugees.

And here's the worst part of all of it: PTSD is curable. Not just manageable and treatable through medication, but actually curable through therapy. You can get better. PTSD should not even really be considered as a "mental health" issue at all- it is closer in nature to a physical injury than an organically occurring chemical disorder of the mind. All of the people who were being discharged to spend the rest of their lives in a waking nightmare could have been spared the misery if they had just been able to access proper trauma therapy.

Eye Movement Desensitization and Reprocessing (EMDR) is an evidenced-based therapy that gently supports people with PTSD to return to the traumatic memories and process them so that they can be filed away correctly. The memories lose the erroneous emotions attached to them. They cease to be 'live' experiences and return to their correct place in the past. It has been tremendously effective in treating combat veterans, victims of sexual abuse and victims of torture.

Refugees and asylum seekers do not just need a safe country to claim asylum. They also need help to find a safe place in their own minds so that they really can build a new life.

This book opens with a quote from Saleh: "If you just speak with me one word, you will hear a million words back." I chose that because it seemed appropriate for a book collecting people's stories, but he was actually talking about therapy. "We need to talk," he continues, "we need someone to listen to us."

Dehumanisation

I just want to say that we are still humans, we still have the rights to live. Being refugees doesn't mean that we have less rights than the normal people. That's just wrong. And going back to Syria wouldn't be the best thing to do now. Not only for Syria, for even other countries that are in danger.

Yezda

The British people are so fabulous. It is the system that is bad.

And there is this term "illegal immigrant." There's a word in English called a euphemism. I never called anyone an illegal immigrant. This is an English country. I studied English. The way you can call somebody is important. You could call somebody "undocumented migrants," or simply "migrant," but they give us this appellation and then there are people who will pick on that.

I look at asylum seekers who are denigrated human beings. "They don't deserve a life" and ,"Oh, they come here, they are economic migrants." It's the way you call people that makes them suitable and makes them accepted in society.

We need to change this appellation and the way they call them.

John

When are you an asylum seeker, they don't treat you as a human being. They think that you come here to their country but you're not allowed to come here.

June

That's what I call that the dehumanisation of refugees. How would you feel? How would any individual feel if you were kept within the fences of a refugee camp? A completely impoverished refugee camp with no resources, with no internet with no even clean water? How would you feel if you were born with that, and live for the rest of your life in that situation?

And that has been the case for many refugees. We have to understand how the 'human' in the 'human rights' is differentially produced, for us to understand what the human rights work is, what the humanitarian work is.

These things are a continuation of the civilising mission of the colonial structures. And the world order itself is built on colonial structures. And the world order that we see today produces the 'human' in various differential ways: some humans are more worthy than others. And some humans are not even humans. They are less than humans, like refugees and asylum seekers, because they are kept from the sphere of humanity itself.

And how can you talk about human rights for refugees and human rights when you're pushing them back in the Mediterranean Sea to die in the international waters outside of the state territorial waters?

How can you say if we are humans or refugees, if states are using all their structures like the violent borders and other structures to keep refugees in isolated spaces where they're completely impoverished?

Are they still humans? Are they still human beings in those carceral spaces? Are they're still human beings in the inflatable ball-like borders, in the middle of the Mediterranean Sea, where they are denied of being even rescued and brought to life?

These to me are the necro-political kinds of experimentation which are basically the politics of death, what's happening outside of the parameters of the state protection. You've already negated their humanity. Basically, what's left is their corporeal self: the body, which is exploitable, deportable and that you can remove anytime. So they don't have any right. And you can do this with impunity.

And that's what happening with refugees and asylum seekers.

To understand that situation of refugees in the UK, one has to understand the physical and non-physical trajectory of the hostile environment to me. The design of the hostile environment's features like immigration detention, unlawful refusal of asylum claims, forced eviction, forced removals, and abject destitution as well within the asylum system. It is deliberately designed to discourage irregular migrants from coming to the UK to seek refuge. But leaving aside the government's rhetoric, the primary goal of creating the hostile environment is apparently to use power to disempower, discourage and expel the so-called undesirable migrants.

And then it spreads throughout the community, through the entire country. That's why I say like, it's the state that has become the carceral, incarceration in the prison is not the cage that we should call the carceral nowadays. And we are in a world where borders are fixed in our bodies, where borders are in our fingerprints, in our eyes and in our face.

To me, personally, when you have that kind of border, biometrics and other borders, and electronic borders, fixed in your body, what it basically tell us is that the government is telling you: I can't trust what you say, but I can trust what your body reveals, what your body tells me, what your fingerprints tells me.

Every time I have been outside of the UK for fieldwork or anything, I always had to wait in the airport with a travel document for two to three hours. And they would question me but they wouldn't trust my responses. And they would ask me to give a fingerprints and check my iris, my documents, and that kind of stuff to crosscheck them with what I was telling them. So that basically felt like they never wanted to trust me. What they trust is the fingerprints, my body. That's why they are controlling my body.

You don't have any agency but the state agency is fixed in your body. So the state's information, the state's powers and relations, are fixed on your body and you're not anything. You're just a vessel.

Yusef

I think human nature likes to put peoples in different bins and buckets. That is just our nature to sort of understand what's out there. Because if we don't do that, we feel insecure. So it's the easiest way to look like someone's in the American bucket and so on. What I tell folks, when I give my talks is that are doorknobs in Damascus and Aleppo that are older than America! [laughs]

So put that in perspective. And now tell me who's the immigrant, right?

Mo

My view is that human rights is ingrained in our DNA. As human beings, human rights has been part of us since the beginning of time.

My understanding is that human rights derive from relationships between individuals. So as long as those relationships are in existence, so it means that human rights are also in existence. And so as long as humans exist, so human rights exist.

So it is not a foreign concept, especially within the context of Kenya, because in Kenya, there has been contestations in many, many, many areas, and for a very long time. So it is not a foreign concept as far as I am concerned.

Idris

Dehumanisation- Notes

Alex Mvuka Ntung is a research consultant and expert in peace-building. He was born in the remote forests of the DRC's borderlands. His family were caught up in the Rwandan genocide in 1994, when a million Tutsis were murdered over a period of just 100 days.

I first met Alex about fifteen years ago, when he was working to help refugees to access higher education. He was always happy and positive, and you couldn't help but warm to him, but his life had been full of suffering. I found out more about it when Alex published his story in 2013: Not My Worst Day, 'a personal journey through violence in the Great Lakes Region of Africa' (Ears Press). It is recommended reading.

Alex took me to a memorial event for the survivors of the Gatumba refugee camp, a massacre when hundreds of Tutsi ethnicity Banyamulenge refugees were shot by the Forces for National Liberation. It was heartbreaking to hear first hand witness testimonies of what happened, and we all prayed it would never happen again.

In 2021, Alex's sister Angelina was murdered by the DRC army. Banyamulenge villages are being burnt, crops are being destroyed and people are being massacred, all while the world is looking elsewhere.

I wanted to understand why this had happened and so I put together a panel of experts for a special radio programme about the situation. One of the people I interviewed was Dr Gregory Stanton, the former Research Professor in Genocide Studies and Prevention at the George Mason University. Dr Stanton previously worked in the US State Department and he was one of the people responsible for bringing the Khmer Rouge to justice. He explained to me that dehumanisation is the process of one group of people denying that another group of people are really human. He has published his theory that there are ten stages of genocide, and that dehumanisation is a key point in enabling persecutors to feel no remorse about their actions. If they are not human then they are just animals or insects, like the "cockroaches" of the propaganda broadcasts in the Rwandan genocide.

Stage	Characteristics
1 Classification	People are divided into 'them' and 'us'.
2 Symbolisation	Symbols of hatred are forced upon unwilling members of pariah groups.
3 Discrimination	Laws exclude groups from full civil-rights. There is segregation or apartheid laws and denial of voting rights.
4 Dehumanisation	One group denies the humanity of the other. Members of it are equated with animals, vermin, insects, or diseases.
5 Organisation	Special army units or militias are trained and armed.
6 Polarisation	Hate groups broadcast polarising propaganda.
7 Preparation	Mass killing is planned. Victims are identified and separated out because of their ethnic or religious identity.
8 Persecution	Expropriation, forced displacement, ghettos, concentration camps.
9 Extermination	It is 'extermination' to the killers because they do not believe their victims to be fully human.
10 Denial	The perpetrators deny that they committed any crimes.

The Ten Stages of Genocide, Gregory Stanton (Genocide Watch) 2012.

The stages are present in every genocide studied, and each stage is a red flag for the future. Neuroscience research shows that the cognitive process of dehumanisation deactivates the regions of our brain associated with empathy and activates the regions associated with disgust (Fiske, S. 2009. 'From Dehumanization and Objectification, to Rehumanization: Neuroimaging Studies on the Building Blocks of Empathy', Annals of the New York Academy of Sciences). Interestingly, political-psychologists repeatedly find that conservatives show higher disgust-sensitivity than liberals (Elad-Strenger, J. et al. 2020. 'Is Disgust a "Conservative" Emotion?', Personality and Social Psychology Bulletin).

The process of equating one group with vermin and diseases is supported by the kind of direct rhetoric such as Daily Mail headlines like "The Swarm on the Streets," or Daily Express front pages such as "Send in Army to Halt Migrant Invasion," "Immigrants Ruining British Way of Life," "Migrants Rob Young Britons of Jobs", "Workers are Fired for Being British", "Migrants Milking Britain's Benefits", or the front pages of The Sun that shouted "Halt the Asylum Tide NOW."

In 2015, The Sun published a column which called refugees "cockroaches". It said they were viruses. It suggested using gunboats to attack migrants in the sea and said that the UK was "plagued by swarms of migrants". This is a newspaper that sells over a million copies a day.

The common photograph of groups of refugees on boats is part of the visual framing of dehumanisation- showing them as a faceless mass rather than individual humans (Bleiker, R et al. 2013. 'The Visual Dehumanisation of Refugees. Australian Journal of Political Science).

The consequences of this process go beyond simply making one group of people feel good about themselves at the expense of another: the more one group feels dehumanised by persecutors, the more they will dehumanise them in return, and the less likely they are to report suspicious or extremist activities in their communities (Kteilly, N. and Bruneau, E. 2017. 'Backlash: The Politics and Real-World Consequences of Minority Group Dehumanization', Personality and Social Psychology Bulletin). The kind of dehumanisation that our respondents recount is counterproductive to social goals of integration and community harmony. It can serve to alienate people irrespective of whether their asylum claims are successful and, in the worst scenarios, is a building block to far worse discrimination in the future.

Hopes for the future

The only thing remaining is if my daughter she can join me. So then my life will be completed. So then I can be growing old and I see my daughter is growing older as well. So we can have a lot of jokes and love. And I can buy chocolate for her.

And she can meet even my other daughter who lives here. So that's what I'm waiting for. Yeah, for eight years. It's a very long time. But I'm just waiting, you know? Like, I have the word like, "never give up."

I'll keep trying.

Maybe one day, one time, I can have that. We can be here hugging each other. "Oh, how are you? Wake up, go and brush your teeth. Make your bed." I can't wait for that.

Paul

I've been asked: should I stay, or should I leave, if I have the chance? And if I had the choice to make, I would definitely stay here, because I wouldn't think that there is a better place for me to stand in apart from the UK. That's kind of my story.

As a refugee, we didn't really choose to come here. We had to. The situations and the conditions in our country made us have to come to here. So if they want us to come back, they need to make sure that we're safe. Because at the end, we are part of the community in here, and even though we're not a complete part, we are kind of a little part. So I think that if you want to come back to Syria, it might look that the war is finished and Syria is safe again, but actually it is not, because they're only believing what there is on the news. And that's not the truth, because I still have my family in Syria. And I do exactly know what's going on there. So I think going back to Syria wouldn't be the best choice that we can make, or the government will make.

Yezda

Hiraeth is a Welsh word that I did not find an exact translation to its meaning in English, but the meaning of *hiraeth* was: extreme homesickness to a homeland or a home that have existed and no longer exists, or might have never existed.

Hopes for the future- Notes

"What are your hopes for the future?" is often the final question we ask on the radio show and podcast.

Asylum seekers face an uncertain future, with the decision on their claim still in the hands of the Home Office, and people with PTSD often struggle to picture themselves in the future at all, so it feels like a good exercise to think of positive visions for the future. It is this spirit of hope and resilience that keeps us all going in the face of adversity and against what are sometimes impossible odds. In the words of our respondent, Idris: "Learn to be a permanent prisoner of hope."

Refugee Radio runs a mental-health support group for refugees and asylum seekers with PTSD. Every week, we start the meeting by running through the ground rules. The ethos behind the group is that it should be led by the needs of the people who attend, so the ground rules have all been devised collaboratively as a group. The rules are mostly the kinds of things that you would expect to see: put your mobile on silent, try to turn up on time, don't discriminate against anyone because of their religion or sexuality etc. But the last rule is my favourite. Every week when we say it, the people in the group will chant it back. Nobody asked them to. It just started organically. There is something about the rule that encapsulates the spirit of the group and our refusal to be ground down by the system or to give in to thoughts of despair or suicide. It is the best rule we could have for the future: "Never give up."

Never give up.